Jaw Breakers and Heart Thumpers

AUTHORS

Barry Courtney
Helen Crossley
Susan Dixon
Loretta Hill
Judith Hillen
Kathleen House

Anne Rudig
Ann Wiebe
Gina Wiens
Nancy Williams
Dave Youngs

EDITORS

Betty Cordel
Judith Hillen
Michelle Pauls
Ann Wiebe

ILLUSTRATORS

Benjamin Hernandez
Reneé Mason
Margo Pocock
Brenda Wood

DESKTOP PUBLISHERS

Tracey Lieder
Kristy Shuler-Russell

Education Foundation

This book contains materials developed by the AIMS Education Foundation. **AIMS** (**A**ctivities **I**ntegrating **M**athematics and **S**cience) began in 1981 with a grant from the National Science Foundation. The non-profit AIMS Education Foundation publishes hands-on instructional materials (books and the quarterly magazine) that integrate curricular disciplines such as mathematics, science, language arts, and social studies. The Foundation sponsors a national program of professional development through which educators may gain both an understanding of the AIMS philosophy and expertise in teaching by integrated, hands-on methods.

ISBN: 978-1-881431-60-2

Printed in the United States of America

Jaw Breakers and Heart Thumpers

TABLE OF CONTENTS

Human Body

Foods

I Hear and I Forget

I See and I Remember

I Do and I Understand

-Chinese Proverb

Project 2061 Benchmarks*

The Nature of Science

- Results of similar scientific investigations seldom turn out exactly the same. Sometimes this is because of unexpected differences in the things being investigated, sometimes because of unrealized differences in the methods used or in the circumstances in which the investigation is carried out, and sometimes just because of uncertainties in observations. It is not always easy to tell which.
- Tools such as thermometers, magnifiers, rulers, or balances often give more information about things than can be obtained by just observing things without their help.
- Science is an adventure that people everywhere can take part in, as they have for many centuries.

The Nature of Mathematics

- Mathematics is the study of many kinds of patterns, including numbers and shapes and operations on them. Sometimes patterns are studied because they help to explain how the world works or how to solve practical problems, sometimes because they are interesting in themselves.

The Nature of Technology

- Measuring instruments can be used to gather accurate information for making scientific comparisons of objects and events and for designing and constructing things that will work properly.

The Physical Setting

- No matter how parts of an object are assembled, the weight of the whole object made is always the same as the sum of the parts; and when a thing is broken into parts, the parts have the same total weight as the original thing.

The Living Environment

- Features used for grouping depend on the purpose of the grouping.
- There is variation among individuals of one kind within a population.
- Some likenesses between children and parents, such as eye color in human beings, or fruit or flower color in plants, are inherited. Other likenesses, such as people's table manners or carpentry skills, are learned.

The Human Organism

- People need water, food, air, waste removal, and a particular range of temperatures in their environment, just as other animals do.
- Food provides energy and materials for growth and repair of body parts. Vitamins and minerals, present in small amounts in foods, are essential to keep everything working well. As people grow up, the amounts and kinds of food and exercise needed by the body may change.
- Toxic substances, some dietary habits, and personal behavior may be bad for one's health. Some effects show up right away, others may not show up for many years. Avoiding toxic substances, such as tobacco, and changing dietary habits to reduce the intake of such things as animal fat increases the chances of living longer.
- Physical health can affect people's emotional well-being and vice versa.

The Designed World

- There are normal ranges for body measurements—including temperature, heart rate, and what is in the blood and urine—that help to tell when people are well. Tools, such as thermometers and x-ray machines, provide us clues about what is happening inside the body.

The Mathematical World

- *Measurements are always likely to give slightly different numbers, even if what is being measured stays the same.*
- *Tables and graphs can show how values of one quantity are related to values of another.*
- *Length can be thought of as unit lengths joined together, area as a set of unit squares, and volume as a set of unit cubes.*
- *Graphical display of numbers may make it possible to spot patterns that are not otherwise obvious, such as comparative size and trends.*
- *Areas of irregular shapes can be found by dividing them into squares and triangles.*
- *Spreading data out on a number line helps to see what the extremes are, where they pile up, and where the gaps are. A summary of data includes where the middle is and how much spread is around it.*

Common Themes

- *Geometric figures, number sequences, graphs, diagrams, sketches, number lines, maps, and stories can be used to represent objects, events, and processes in the real world, although such representations can never be exact in every detail.*

- *Things change in steady, repetitive, or irregular ways—or sometimes in more than one way at the same time. Often the best way to tell which kinds of change are happening is to make a table or graph of measurements.*
- *Finding out what the biggest and smallest possible values of something are is often as revealing as knowing what the usual value is.*

Habits of Mind

- *Keep records of their investigations and observations and not change the records later.*
- *Add, subtract, multiply, and divide whole numbers mentally, on paper, and with a calculator.*
- *Make sketches to aid in explaining procedures or ideas.*
- *Use numerical data in describing and comparing objects and events.*
- *Recognize when comparisons might not be fair because some conditions are not kept the same.*

* *American Association for the Advancement of Science. **Benchmarks for Science Literacy**. Oxford University Press. New York. 1993.*

NRC Standards*

Abilities necessary to do scientific inquiry

- Plan and conduct a simple investigation.
- Use data to construct a reasonable explanation.
- Communicate investigations and explanations.
- Employ simple equipment and tools to gather data and extend the senses.
- Use appropriate tools and techniques to gather, analyze, and interpret data.
- Develop descriptions, explanations, predictions, and models using evidence.
- Think critically and logically to make the relationships between evidence and explanations.

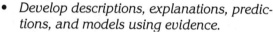

Properties of objects and materials

- Objects have many observable properties, including size, weight, shape, color, temperature, and the ability to react with other substances. Those properties can be measured using tools, such as rulers, balances, and thermometers.

The characteristics of organisms

- Organisms have basic needs. For example, animals need air, water, and food; plants require air, water, nutrients, and light. Organisms can survive only in environments, in which their needs can be met. The world has many different environments and distinct environments support the life of different types of organisms.
- Each plant or animal has different structures that serve different functions in growth, survival, and reproduction. For example, humans have distinct body structures for walking, holding, seeing, and talking.

Understandings about science and technology

- Tools help scientists make better observations, measurements, and equipment for investigations. They help scientists see, measure, and do things that they could not otherwise see, measure and do.

Personal health

- Regular exercise is important to the maintenance and improvement of health. The benefits of physical fitness include maintaining healthy weight, having energy and strength for routine activities, good muscle tone, bone strength, strong heart/lung systems, and improved mental health. Personal exercise, especially developing cardiovascular endurance, is the foundation of physical fitness.
- Nutrition is essential to health. Students should understand how the body uses food and how various foods contribute to health. Recommendations for good nutrition include eating a variety of foods, eating less sugar, and eating less fat.

*   National Research Council. **National Science Education Standards.** National Academy Press. Washington, DC. 1996.

NCTM Standards 2000*

Number and Operations

Understand numbers, ways of representing numbers, relationships among numbers, and number systems
- *develop understanding of fractions as parts of unit wholes, as parts of a collection, as locations on number lines, and as divisions of whole numbers*
- *understand and use ratios and proportions to represent quantitative relationships*

Understand meanings of operations and how they relate to one another
- *understand the effects of multiplying and dividing whole numbers*

Measurement

Understand measurable attributes of objects and the units, systems, and processes of measurement
- *understand such attributes as length, area, weight, volume, and size of angle and select the appropriate type of unit for measuring each attribute*
- *understand that measurements are approximations and how differences in units affect precision*

Apply appropriate techniques, tools, and formulas to determine measurements
- *select and apply appropriate standard units and tools to measure length, area, volume, weight, time, temperature, and the size of angles*
- *select and use benchmarks to estimate measurements*

Data Analysis and Probability

Formulate questions that can be addressed with data and collect, organize, and display relevant data to answer them
- *collect data using observations, surveys, and experiments*
- *represent data using tables and graphs such as line plots, bar graphs, and line graphs*

Select and use appropriate statistical methods to analyze data
- *use measures of center, focusing on the median, and understand what each does and does not indicate about the data set*

Problem Solving
- *solve problems that arise in mathematics and in other contexts*
- *apply and adapt a variety of appropriate strategies to solve problems*

*   *National Council of Teachers of Mathematics.* **Principles and Standards for School Mathematics.** *The National Council of Teachers of Mathematics, Inc. Reston, Virginia. 2000.*

Hands on the Giant

Topic
Proportional reasoning

Key Question
How tall is the giant?

Learning Goal
Students will seek to determine the approximate height of a giant given only an example of a giant hand print.

Guiding Documents
Project 2061 Benchmarks
- *Tools such as thermometers, magnifiers, rulers, or balances often give more information about things than can be obtained by just observing things without their help.*
- *Length can be thought of as unit lengths joined together, area as a collection of unit squares, and volume as a set of unit cubes.*
- *Make sketches to aid in explaining procedures or ideas.*

NRC Standards
- *Use data to construct a reasonable explanation.*
- *Communicate investigations and explanations.*

NCTM Standards 2000*
- *Understand such attributes as length, area, weight, volume, and size of angle and select the appropriate type of unit for measuring each attribute*
- *Understand that measurements are approximations and understand how differences in units affect precision*
- *Select and use benchmarks to estimate measurements*
- *Understand and use ratios and proportions to represent quantitative relationships*
- *Solve problems that arise in mathematics and in other contexts*
- *Apply and adapt a variety of appropriate strategies to solve problems*

Math
Measurement
    length
Ratio and proportion
Estimation
Problem solving

Science
Life science
    human body ratios

Integrated Processes
Predicting
Observing
Comparing and contrasting
Collecting and recording data
Interpreting data
Generalizing
Applying

Materials
Large chart paper or butcher paper
Tools for measuring length such as rulers, metric tape
    measures, meter sticks
Non-standard measurement tools such as chalkboard
    erasers or pencils
Scissors
Colored markers
Paper hand print of the giant's hand (see *Management 4*)

Background Information
    This problem, when encountered by adult learners, seems to signal the immediate use of a proportional equation such as—the measure of my hand is to the measure of my height as the measure of the giant's hand is to X (the measure of the giant's height). Cross multiply and solve for X.

    It may be more enlightening to have students avoid using a proportional equation, even if they know how, and solve the problem by *doing* it in some other way.

    The problem focuses on the application of *proportional reasoning* that underlies the ultimate proportional equation. The power of this activity is in the multiple responses one can observe in a classroom and how it helps to convey what students know and understand about proportional reasoning. The emphasis is on looking at how students communicate what they know (or do not know).

The focus is *not* that students use the same unit of measure to express their answers or that they even use a standard unit. Very young students have solved the problem by suggesting the giant is 10 giant hands tall based on the idea that they could use their own hand (laid end to end) to measure their own height and that the giant must be the same number of hands tall. Their answer of 10 giant hands is valid *with that explanation*. Other students reason that if the giant's hand is three times bigger than their hand, then the giant must be three times taller, or three students tall.

Notice that it is appropriate to compare the student's hand to the giant's hand and the student's height to the giant's height. It also makes sense to compare the student's hand to the student's height and the giant's hand to the giant's height. The giant's height can be expressed in number of student hands, number of giant hands, number of student heights, or in some standard unit of measure such as centimeters, meters, inches, or feet.

Management

1. This experience is intended for small groups of three or four students.
2. Each group should use one large piece of chart paper to picture and write about how they solved the problem.
3. Encourage students to use words, pictures, and symbols to show their thinking and what they did to find out how tall the giant was. Examples of four different responses, representing a composite of student explanations, have been included for teacher reference only.
4. To make the giant's hand, use a marker to draw around your hand on a transparency. Put the transparency on the overhead projector, trace the outline on newsprint or other paper, and cut it out. Use this pattern to make one giant hand for each group.

Procedure

1. Introduce the problem with this scenario: *During the night, a giant entered our classroom and, while groping in the dark for the light switch, the giant left a large smudge that looked like a hand print on the wall. Not wishing to leave this mark for someone else to clean up, I began to remove its trace from the wall when suddenly I began to wonder how tall this giant could be. I quickly made a paper copy of the giant's hand print. Can you help me find the approximate height of the giant?*

2. Distribute a giant hand print and a large piece of chart paper to each group of students. Make available the measurement devices listed.
3. Instruct the groups to use the large chart paper to show how they solved the problem, including the question and a step-by-step description of what they did. They should use words, pictures, symbols, and numbers to explain their thinking.
4. Have each group share its solution with the rest of the class.
5. Give each student the activity page for independent reflection and response. Three questions are included: What did you learn? What mathematics did you do? How did you feel about the problem and finding a solution?

Connecting Learning

1. How many different ways are there to find the height of the giant? Describe them.
2. What does it mean to measure a *hand?* [length of hand or width of hand]
3. How are hands used to measure height? [laid end to end or side by side]
4. What other ways of measuring were used? How did they affect the answer?
5. Could this giant stand up in our room? If we asked the giant to lie down on the floor, show me where his feet would be and how far away his head would be.
6. What assumptions did your group make to solve the problem? [that the hand to height relationship of the giant was similar to that of a student]
7. What changes in procedure were made by your group as you worked to solve the problem? What procedures did not work?
8. How are you sure that your estimate of the giant's height is fairly accurate?
9. What kinds of mathematics did you use in solving the problem?

Extension

Distribute a tiny hand print and ask students to consider finding the approximate height of a mini-person. Is the process the same or different?

*   Reprinted with permission from *Principles and Standards for School Mathematics*, 2000 by the National Council of Teachers of Mathematics. All rights reserved.

How big is the giant?

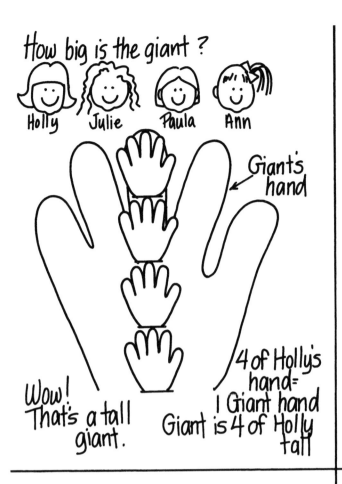

Holly Julie Paula Ann

Giant's hand

Wow! That's a tall giant.

4 of Holly's hand = 1 Giant hand
Giant is 4 of Holly tall

How tall is the giant?

A student lies down on the ground. Draw a line at the top of his head and bottom of feet. Student takes his hand to measure his height in hands.

Steve is 10 of his own hands tall.

So the giant is 10 giant hands tall

Use giant's hands — hand over hand to find out how tall the giant is.

How tall is the giant?

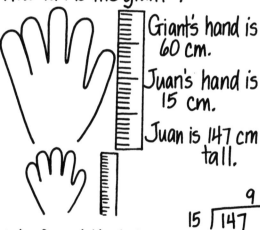

Giant's hand is 60 cm.

Juan's hand is 15 cm.

Juan is 147 cm tall.

$$\begin{array}{r} 9 \\ 15\overline{)147} \\ 135 \\ \hline 12 \end{array}$$

We found that Juan is almost 10 hands tall.

So the giant is 10 times taller than his hand.

600 cm tall

How tall is the giant?

Have Tasha stand by the wall and mark her height. Use her hands to find how many hands tall she is. (9½)

Mark a beginning point on floor. Move the giant's hand end to end on the floor and mark the place for 9½ giant hands.

Use measuring tape to find how tall giant is. (570 cm)

Hands on the Giant

Key Question

How tall is the giant?

Learning Goal

Students will:

seek to determine the approximate height of a giant given only an example of a giant hand print.

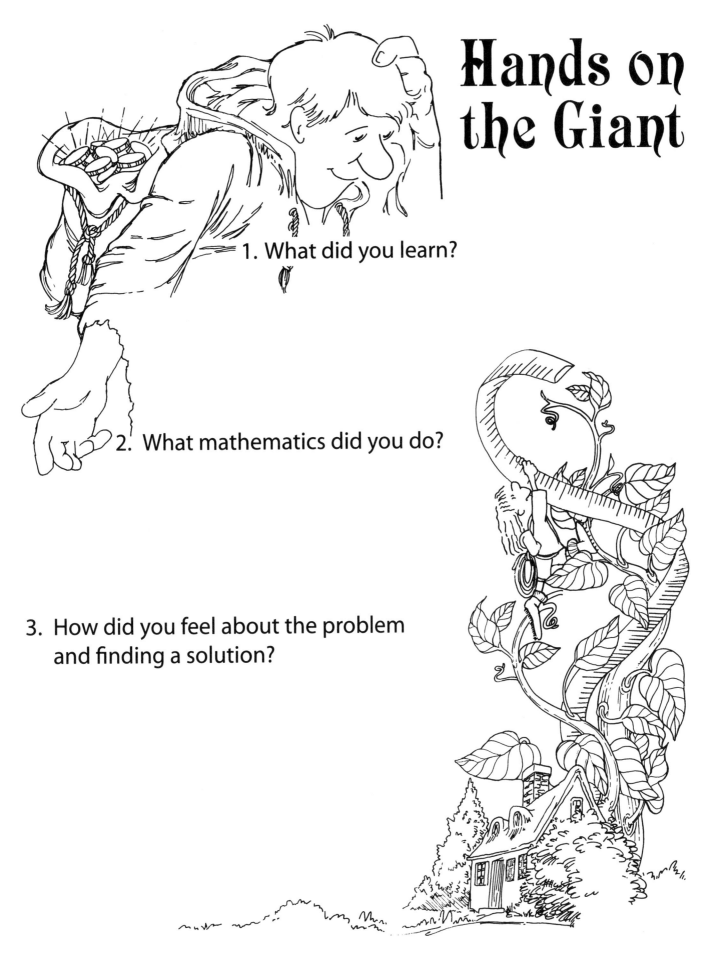

Hands on the Giant

1. What did you learn?

2. What mathematics did you do?

3. How did you feel about the problem and finding a solution?

Hands on the Giant

Connecting Learning

1. How many different ways are there to find the height of the giant? Describe them.

2. What does it mean to measure a *hand?*

3. How are hands used to measure height?

4. What other ways of measuring were used? How did they affect the answer?

5. Could this giant stand up in our room? If we asked the giant to lie down on the floor, show me where his feet would be and how far away his head would be.

6. What assumptions did your group make to solve the problem?

Hands on the Giant

Connecting Learning

7. What changes in procedure were made by your group as you worked to solve the problem? What procedures did not work?

8. How are you sure that your estimate of the giant's height is fairly accurate?

9. What kinds of mathematics did you use in solving the problem?

Topic
Body ratios: head circumference to height

Key Question
How does your height compare to the circumference of your head?

Learning Goal
Students will explore the relationship between their heights and the circumferencees of their heads.

Guiding Documents
Project 2061 Benchmarks
- *Mathematics is the study of many kinds of patterns, including numbers and shapes and operations on them. Sometimes patterns are studied because they help to explain how the world works or how to solve practical problems, sometimes because they are interesting in themselves.*
- *Tables and graphs can show how values of one quantity are related to values of another.*

NRC Standards
- *Plan and conduct a simple investigation.*
- *Employ simple equipment and tools to gather data and extend the senses.*
- *Use data to construct a reasonable explanation.*

NCTM Standards 2000*
- *Understand such attributes as length, area, weight, volume, and size of angle and select the appropriate type of unit for measuring each attribute*
- *Select and apply appropriate standard units and tools to measure length, area, volume, weight, time, temperature, and the size of angles*
- *Collect data using observations, surveys, and experiments*
- *Represent data using tables and graphs such as line plots, bar graphs, and line graphs*
- *Use measures of center, focusing on the median, and understand what each does and does not indicate about the data set*

Math
Estimation
Measurement
   length
Averages
Ratios

Science
Life science
   human body

Integrated Processes
Predicting
Observing
Collecting and recording data
Controlling variables
Hypothesizing
Interpreting data
Comparing and contrasting
Generalizing
Applying

Materials
Metric tape measures or string and meter sticks
Calculators

Background Information
This activity explores one of the surprising ratios evident in the human body. How many times greater is your height than your head circumference? When asked this question, many adults guess that their heights are between four to eight times greater. The actual adult ratio is about 3 to 1 (height is 3 times greater than 1 head circumference). This is quite amazing to many people since they do not have a good intuitive feel for circumferences and tend to underestimate them.

The vast majority of adults will find that their heights are between 2.8-3.2 times greater than their head circumferences. If a large group is sampled, the average will be quite close to 3.0.

Age is an important factor in the height to head ratio. The ratio for infants is about 2 to 1. As children mature, their ratios change continually until they reach their adult ratios sometime after puberty. The ratios for most elementary school children will fall in the range of about 2.4-2.8 to 1, depending on their ages.

Management
Students should measure their heights and head circumferences to the nearest centimeter. They need to measure accurately, taking care to measure their heads at the largest circumference (usually right above the ears and eyes) and to measure their heights while standing up straight with shoes removed. The height/head circumference ratios should to be rounded to the nearest tenth.

(The alternate approaches that follow are offered for those teachers whose students are ready for more independent investigations.)

Open-ended: Ask the *Key Question* and let student groups plan how they will answer it. When students finish, have them report their findings.

Guided planning: Ask the *Key Question.* Encourage groups to develop a procedure for finding the answer, giving guidance as needed. Help students deal with such things as accuracy of measurement, controlling variables, using calculators, rounding results to the nearest tenth, and finding group and class averages.

Procedure

1. Ask the *Key Question* and distribute the first two activity pages.
2. Have students predict how many times greater their heights are than the circumferences of their heads and record these predictions (to the nearest whole number) on the first activity sheet. Optional: Make a class tally of the predictions so they can later be compared with the results.
3. Discuss how to take accurate measurements with the tape measures and round calculator computations to the nearest tenth.
4. Have students work in groups of four to six. Each student should record the group results on the top of the second activity page.
5. After all groups have found their averages, have students share **group totals** (not averages), complete the class chart, and calculate the class averages based on the total number of people who participated.
6. Discuss the results.
7. Challenge students to apply the knowledge they have gained by doing the activities at the bottom of the first page. Have each group measure the height of one person from another group and predict that person's head circumference. Measure the circumference and compare. Have each group pick another person and measure that person's head circumference and predict his/her height. Measure the height and compare.
8. Extend this activity by challenging students to think of related questions that they might ask. The third activity page lists several questions to stimulate discussion. Have students choose a question to explore, state their hypothesis, devise and carry out a plan to test their hypothesis, and report the results.

Connecting Learning

1. Were you close in your prediction of how many times greater your height was than the circumference of your head? Explain.
2. Is there a close relationship between height and circumference of the head? What is that relationship?
3. Would one person be a good sample? Explain. (pick individual statistics and check)
4. How many people do you think would make a good sample? Why do you think this?
5. Compare your group averages to the class averages. Which do you think are more accurate? [class averages] Why? [The larger the sample, the more accurate the results.]
6. Does the ratio change with age, gender, or height of the person measured? How could you test this?
7. Are there patterns that you noticed in this activity? Explain.
8. Can you come close to predicting someone's height knowing the circumference of their head or vice versa? Explain.
9. What hypothesis did you make?
10. What were your results?
11. What are you wondering now?

Extensions

1. Have students construct graphs of data.
2. Students might want to explore other ratios found in the human body.

Home Link

Have students measure the heights and head circumferences of family members and share this data with the class. In this way, students could collect data on adult ratios and ratios for other ages of children.

* Reprinted with permission from *Principles and Standards for School Mathematics,* 2000 by the National Council of Teachers of Mathematics. All rights reserved.

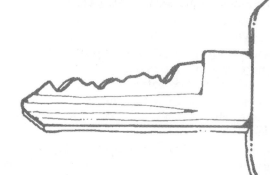

Now That's Using Your Head!

Key Question

How does your height compare to the circumference of your head?

Learning Goals

Students will:

- explore the relationship between their heights and the circumferences of their heads, and

- draw conclusions about the heights to circumference ratio.

Now That's Using Your Head!

How does your height compare to the circumference of your head?

I predict my height is _____ times greater than the circumference of my head.

SUMMARY OF RESULTS

1. **My height** is actually _____ times greater than the circumference of my head.
2. My **group's average height** is _____ times greater than the average circumference.
3. The **class' average height** is _____ times greater than the average circumference.

APPLICATION

Measure the head circumference of someone whose height you do not know. Predict their height. Check your prediction by measuring.

Measure the height of someone whose head circumference you do not know. Predict their head circumference. Check your prediction by measuring.

Now That's Using Your Head!

Group Table

Name	Height (cm)	Circumference of Head (cm)	Times greater (Ht. ÷ Circum.)
Totals			

Averages _____   _____   _____

Class Table

Name	# of people	Group Totals Height (cm)	Circumference of Head (cm)	Times greater (Ht. ÷ Circum.)
Totals				

Averages _____   _____   _____

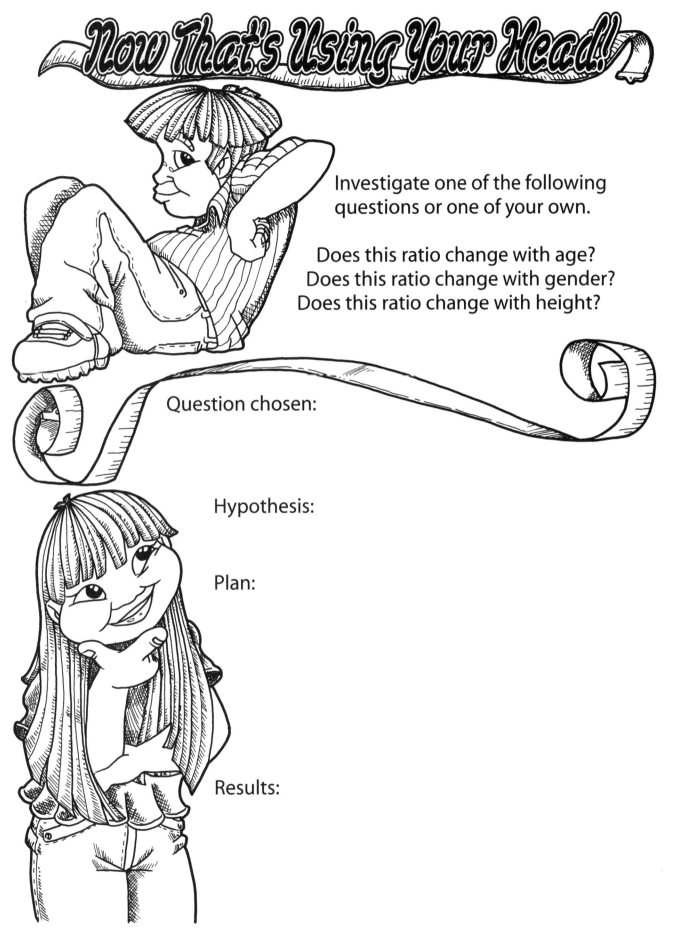

Now That's Using Your Head!

Investigate one of the following questions or one of your own.

Does this ratio change with age?
Does this ratio change with gender?
Does this ratio change with height?

Question chosen:

Hypothesis:

Plan:

Results:

Connecting Learning

1. Were you close in your prediction of how many times greater your height was than the circumference of your head? Explain.

2. Is there a close relationship between height and circumference of the head? What is that relationship?

3. Would one person be a good sample? Explain.

4. How many people do your think would make a good sample? Why do you think this?

5. Compare your group averages to the class averages. Which do you think are more accurate? Why?

Connecting Learning

6. Does the ratio change with age, gender, or height of the person measured? How could you test this?

7. Are there patterns that you noticed in this activity? Explain.

8. Can you come close to predicting someone's height knowing the circumference of their head or vice versa? Explain.

9. What hypothesis did you make?

10. What were the results?

11. What are you wondering now?

How do you Measure Up?

Topic
Body ratios: femur length to height

Key Question
How is your longest bone related to your height?

Learning Goal
Students will discover how femur length is related to total height.

Guiding Documents
Project 2061 Benchmarks
- *Measurements are always likely to give slightly different numbers, even if what is being measured stays the same.*
- *Use numerical data in describing and comparing objects and events.*

NRC Standards
- *Employ simple equipment and tools to gather data and extend the senses.*
- *Communicate investigations and explanations.*

NCTM Standards 2000*
- *Collect data using observations, surveys, and experiments*
- *Understand such attributes as length, area, weight, volume, and size of angle and select the appropriate type of unit for measuring each attribute*
- *Understand that measurements are approximations and understand how differences in units affect precision*
- *Select and use benchmarks to estimate measurements*
- *Understand and use ratios and proportions to represent quantitative relationships*
- *Solve problems that arise in mathematics and in other contexts*

Math
Estimation
  rounding
Measurement
  length
Percent

Science
Life science
  human body

Integrated Processes
Observing
Estimating
Collecting and recording data
Comparing
Generalizing

Materials
For each student:
  1 piece of masking tape
  1 piece of construction paper, 2" x 18"
  crayons
  metric ruler

For the class:
  meter sticks
  calculators
  chart-size graphing grid (see *Management 4*)

Background Information
With a single bone, anthropologists can often estimate the height of a person who lived a long time ago. This is possible because there are relationships between the lengths of the major bones (humerus, radius, femur, and tibia) and a person's height.

The femur, the thigh bone, is the longest bone in the human body. Roughly four femur lengths equal a person's height. For an average adult the femur length will be about 27% of their height, for elementary students about 25%. There are, however, variations between males and females and in the accuracy of measurements. Here is another way to figure this relationship:

Males: (1.9 x femur length) + 81.3 cm
Females: (1.9 x femur length) + 72.8 cm

Management
1. Recruit at least two adults or cross-age tutors to assist with measuring heights and femur lengths. If more helpers are available, the class can be divided into smaller measuring groups.
2. Measurements are never exact, but those of the femur tend to vary more in accuracy because it cannot be seen externally.
3. Cut 2" x 18" pieces of colored construction paper, one for each student.

4. Enlarge the large graphing grid provided or recreate it on chart paper for recording the percentage results of the class. You will need to fill in the appropriate numbers to reflect the range of percentages your students calculate.
5. If the concept and calculation of percent are not appropriate for your class, the investigation can be completed by relating the number of femur lengths to height as noted in *Procedure 6* and *7*.

Procedure

1. Ask students, "What do you think is the longest bone in your body?" After some discussion, distribute the activity page and look at the skeleton for further clues.
2. Ask the *Key Question* and record a sampling of student responses. Estimates may be expressed as the number of femurs that equal their height or as a percentage of their height.
3. With adult supervision, have one group of students help each other measure and record their heights without shoes. Each student should write his or her name on a piece of tape and place it on the wall to mark his or her height.
4. At the same time, another group should measure and record their femur lengths. To measure, have the student sit up straight in a chair. Using a meter stick, measure the horizontal length of the femur bone from the back of the hip to the front of the knee.
5. Distribute the construction paper strips and have each student measure and cut it the same length as their femur.
6. Students should take their construction paper strips to their height mark and count the approximate number of femur lengths that fit into their height.
7. Instruct students to write their results on the activity page.
8. Distribute calculators and have students determine the percentage and record the procedure on the activity page. Have them round to the nearest centimeter (or millimeter if you want to work with decimals).
9. Instruct students to complete the percentage graph by coloring it in up to the point that corresponds to their percent.
10. Display the class graph. Determine and label the range. Expect a range around 23% to 28% because accurate femur measurement is somewhat difficult.
11. Have students come to the front and color a square in the column that corresponds to their percent.
12. Discuss and compare class graph results. Make generalizations.

Connecting Learning

1. What do you think is the longest bone in your body? [thigh bone or femur]
2. Which was easier to measure, your height or your femur? [height] Why? [Height is an external measurement; your feet and head form physical boundaries for the measuring tool. The femur is internal so we have to guess where it starts and ends.]
3. How accurate do you think our measurements are? [Height should be more accurate than femur length for the reasons stated in the preceding answer.]
4. How does your percent compare with others in the class?
5. What statements can be made from the graph?
6. Are the results the same for boys as they are for girls? (Separate the boy's results from the girl's results and examine. See *Background Information*.)
7. Do you think there is a relationship between other pairs of body measurements? (Have students develop hypotheses.) What investigation would you like to plan and test? (Allow them to test their hypotheses at an appropriate time.)

Extensions

1. Have students find the average percentage for the class, also the average for girls and the average for boys. Discuss the range (high and low) in femur measurement and the degree to which it varies from the average.
2. Label a diagram of the human skeleton.
3. Compare and contrast the human skeleton with those of birds and animals.
4. Measure the femur of a pet and compare it to the animal's total body height or length.

Curriculum Correlation

Literature
Parker, Steve. *Skeleton* (Eyewitness Books). Alfred A. Knopf. New York. 1988.

Music
Sing "Bones and More Bones" and/or "Dry Bones."

Art
Make a skeleton or bone mobile.

* Reprinted with permission from *Principles and Standards for School Mathematics*, 2000 by the National Council of Teachers of Mathematics. All rights reserved.

How do you Measure Up?

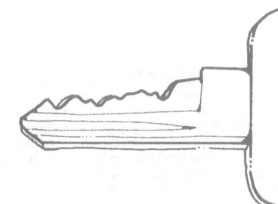

Key Question

How is your longest bone related to your height?

Learning Goal

Students will:

discover how femur length is related to total height.

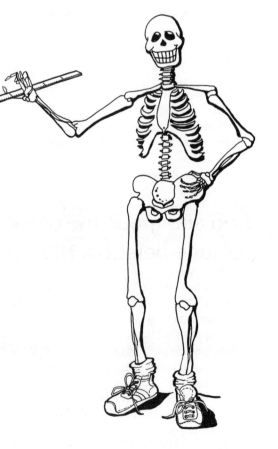

How do you Measure Up?

How is your longest bone related to your height?

Height _____

Femur _____

What did you discover?

Find and graph the percent (femur ÷ height) x 100

Femur Length as a Percent of Height

0   10   20   30   40   50   60   70   80   90   100

How do you Measure Up? Class Graph

Number of Students

Femur Length as a Percent of Height

Bones and More Bones

Words by Suzy Gazlay   Tune: Heads and Shoulders, Knees and Toes

Scap-u-la, ra-di-us, fe-mur, tib-i-a, fe-mur, tib-i-a;

Scap-u-la, ra-di-us, fe-mur, tib-i-a, fe-mur, tib-i-a; Shoul-der

blade, fore- arm and thigh and shin;

Scap-u-la, ra-di-us, fe-mur, tib-i-a, fe-mur, tib-i-a;

Point to the location of various bones as they are named. The song will take on a calisthenic form. Adjust the words to fit the song. For example:

Clavicle, ribs, patella, tarsals; patella, tarsals...
(Collarbone and ribs;
kneecap and anklebones...)

or

Cranium, sternum, metatarsals; metatarsals...
(Top of skull, breastbone,
and down to the feet...)

How do you Measure Up?

Connecting Learning

1. What do you think is the longest bone in your body?

2. Which was easier to measure, your height or your femur? Why?

3. How accurate do you think our measurements are?

4. How does your percent compare with others in the class?

5. What statements can be made from the graph?

6. Are the results the same for boys as they are for girls?

7. Do you think there is a relationship between other pairs of body measurements? What investigation would you like to plan and test?

ARE YOU AN AVERAGE JOE?

Topic
Body size variations

Key Question
How do you compare to the average person in your class?

Learning Goals
Students will:
- find the size of the average person in the class, and
- compare themselves to that average.

Guiding Documents
Project 2061 Benchmarks
- *There is variation among individuals of one kind within a population.*
- *Some likenesses between children and parents, such as eye color in human beings, or fruit or flower color in plants, are inherited. Other likenesses, such as people's table manners or carpentry skills, are learned.*

NRC Standard
- *Employ simple equipment and tools to gather data and extend the senses.*

NCTM Standards 2000*
- *Collect data using observations, surveys, and experiments*
- *Use measures of center, focusing on the median, and understand what each does and does not indicate about the data set*
- *Select and apply appropriate standard units and tools to measure length, area, volume, weight, time, temperature, and the size of angles*
- *Understand that measurements are approximations and understand how differences in units affect precision*
- *Solve problems that arise in mathematics and in other contexts*

Math
Estimation
   rounding
Measurement
   length
Whole number operations
Averages

Science
Life science
   human body

Integrated Processes
Observing
Estimating
Controlling variables
Collecting and recording data
Comparing and contrasting
Generalizing

Materials
Large piece of butcher paper, one per student
Meter tapes, one for every two students
Crayons or markers
Calculators

Background Information
People vary in shape and size. Heredity is one factor influencing this variation. For example, if both parents are short, the offspring will likely be short too. Personal choices about food and exercise are another influence on shape and size. Heredity cannot be changed; food and exercise decisions are controlled by the individual.

Although the types of measurements taken in this activity should not be threatening to most students, class sharing involves the use of partner averages rather than individual measurements to ease the minds of those who are sensitive about their size. Individual comparisons to the class average are intended for personal evaluation.

Management
1. Cut large pieces of butcher paper for body tracings.
2. To make the tracings, arrange to use a large area such as a cafeteria or have successive pairs of students work in the back of the classroom while regular instruction continues. It is best if students wear light rather than bulky clothing during tracing. Tracings can be done at home by sending paper and a pencil home with each child. For easy transport, roll the paper into a tube and secure it with a rubber band.
3. If meter tapes are not available, have students make their own using the tape pattern at the back of this book. Measurements and averages may be rounded to the nearest centimeter or the nearest millimeter.

4. Three class sessions are suggested.
   Part One: Trace bodies and make measurements.
   Part Two: Determine averages and construct the average person.
   Part Three: Compare personal measurements to the class average.
5. Students may associate the word *average*, with someone who earns C's or is less than outstanding. Students should understand that a mathematical average does not have the same connotations. Prior work with averaging is desirable.
6. Be sensitive to students concerned about size.

Procedure

Part One

1. Ask questions such as, "Do you think the students your age are the same size?", "Do you all have the same arm length?", etc. Explain that they will discover the size variations and draw an average student in their class.
2. Give students the activity page and use the illustration to define the beginning and ending points of each measurement. Everyone needs to use the same standards (controlling variables). Head width should be measured at the widest part. For the purposes of this investigation, arm length should be measured from shoulder to the tip of the longest finger and leg length from the bottom of the hip to the foot. Height, head to shoulder, and shoulder to feet measurements should be taken perpendicular to the feet, not at a slant.
3. Divide the class into pairs. Have each pair make estimates for themselves and their partners and record these in the table.
4. Instruct one partner to lie face up on a piece of butcher paper while the other traces his or her body with a pencil, paying careful attention to details such as fingers. Have them go over tracings with crayon or marker and then switch places.
5. Have them take measurements from the tracing and record these on the activity page.

Part Two

1. Instruct partners to find the average measurements for the two of them.
2. With the whole class, add up all partners' averages to get a class average of each measurement.
3. Choose a few students to construct a body drawing based on these average measurements.

Part Three

1. Have students find the difference between their own measurements and the class average. It is easier to calculate and compare differences if students lightly color the *Me* (under Actual) and *Class Average* rows in the table. Discuss the results.

Connecting Learning

1. How much of a variation is there between you and the average? (This may be a written evaluation rather than shared orally with the class.)
2. Which measurements were closest to the class average?
3. Which were furthest from the class average?
4. Who in our class is the closest to our average model?
5. How might the results at another grade level be alike? …different?
6. What things determine your body size? [size of parents (heredity), eating and exercise choices made by the individual]
7. What is good about being short? …medium? …tall?
8. What do you appreciate most about yourself?
9. If the teacher's measurements were included, how would the class average change? (Students might think it would change a lot. It wouldn't because the amount added is being divided by the number of class members.)

Extensions

1. Measure a class at another grade level and construct an average model based on the results.
2. Collect samples of other species, such as leaves or flowers from the same plant, to compare size variations.
3. Have students research normal height ranges for their age group.

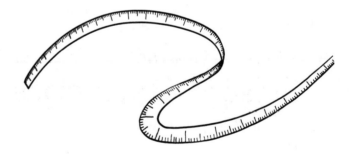

ARE YOU AN AVERAGE JOE?

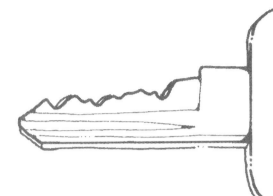

Key Question

How do you compare to the average person in your class?

Learning Goals

Students will:

- find the size of the average person in their class, and

- compare themselves to that average.

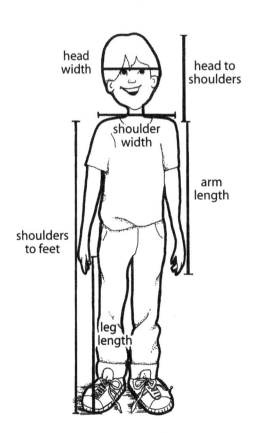

ARE YOU AN AVERAGE JOE?

How do you compare to the average person in your class?

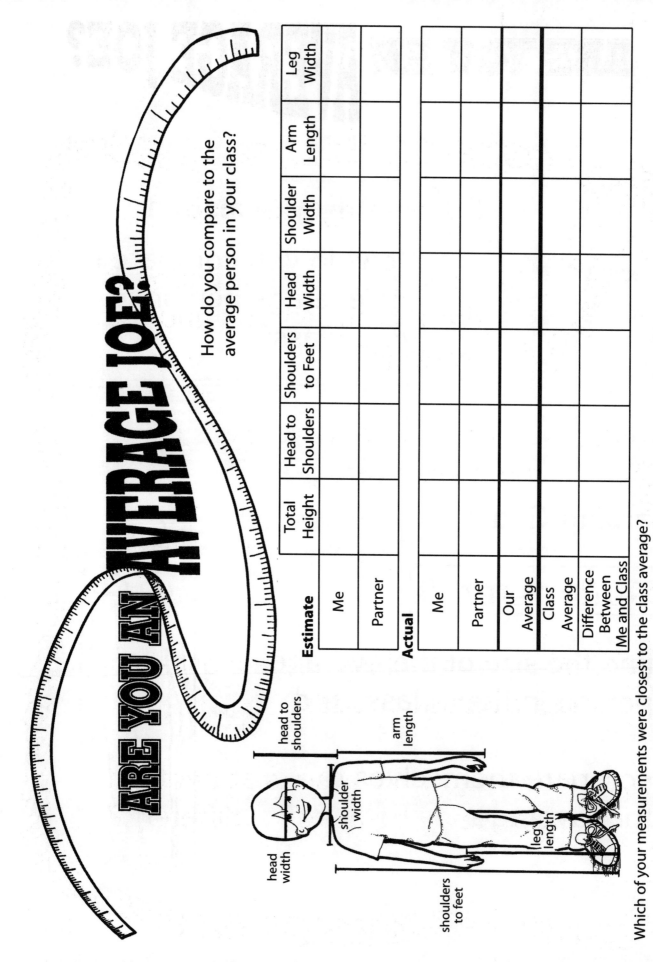

Estimate	Total Height	Head to Shoulders	Shoulders to Feet	Head Width	Shoulder Width	Arm Length	Leg Width
Me							
Partner							

Actual							
Me							
Partner							
Our Average							
Class Average							
Difference Between Me and Class							

head to shoulders

arm length

shoulder width

head width

leg length

shoulders to feet

Which of your measurements were closest to the class average?

Which were furthest from the class average?

ARE YOU AN AVERAGE JOE?

Connecting Learning

1. How much of a variation is there between you and the average?

2. Which measurements were closest to the class average?

3. Which were furthest from the class average?

4. Who in our class is the closest to our average model?

5. How might the results at another grade level be alike? ...different?

ARE YOU AN AVERAGE JOE?

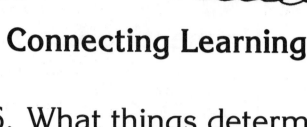

Connecting Learning

6. What things determine your body size?

7. What is good about being short? ...medium? ...tall?

8. What do you appreciate most about yourself?

9. If the teacher's measurements were included, how would the class average change?

OUR BODY OF WATER

Topic
Human body: water content

Key Question
How much of your body is water?

Learning Goals
Students will:
- learn how much water is in their bodies, and
- learn the importance of water in maintaining health.

Guiding Documents
Project 2061 Benchmarks
- *People need water, food, air, waste removal, and a particular range of temperatures in their environment, just as other animals do.*
- *Geometric figures, number sequences, graphs, diagrams, sketches, number lines, maps, and stories can be used to represent objects, events, and processes in the real world, although such representations can never be exact in every detail.*

NRC Standard
- *Organisms have basic needs. For example, animals need air, water, and food; plants require air, water, nutrients, and light. Organisms can survive only in environments, and distinct environments support the life of different types of organisms.*

NCTM Standards 2000*
- *Collect data using observations, surveys, and experiments*
- *Represent data using tables and graphs such as line plots, bar graphs, and line graphs*
- *Solve problems that arise in mathematics and in other contexts*

Math
Measurement
   volume
Whole number operations
Graphs

Science
Life science
   health

Integrated Processes
Observing
Collecting and recording data
Comparing and contrasting
Applying

Materials
1 or more liter containers with deciliter markings
Funnel that fits in two-liter bottle opening
Water source
12 or more two-liter bottles (see *Management 2*)
Scissors
Crayons
Straight edges
Colored rice or barley (see *Management 5*)
Glue
Scale, optional (see *Management 1*)

Background Information
   Those who experience this activity should gain a better understanding of two things. First, a significant part of our bodies is water. Second, water lost through normal body processes must be replaced to maintain good health.

Percentage of Water
   The human body is about 60% or three-fifths water. This is a general average because the percentage of water varies with age and amount of fat. The percentage in infants may be as high as 84, but decreases markedly in the first 10 years of life. As adults, men tend to have higher percentages of water (65-50%) than women (55-40%) because of their greater muscle mass and lower amount of fat. Muscle has more water, fat has very little. The average 70-kg adult male is about 60% water.

   Water is present not only in body fluids but in all kinds of cells, from the bones to the brain. In fact, there is no more water in the blood than in some tissue we think of as *solid*.

Water in Tissues[2]

Skin	70%
Fat	20%
Blood	80%
Muscle (striated)	75%
Connective	60%
Bone	25-30%
Liver	70%
Kidney	80%
Nervous Tissue: Gray	85%
Nervous Tissue: White	70%

Importance of Water
   Water is essential to maintain the human body. It is the medium in which all of the body's chemical reactions take place. Water transports substances such as

nutrients, hormones, oxygen, carbon dioxide, and body wastes. It dilutes toxic substances and helps distribute heat.[1]

Body water is lost through sweat (20%), elimination of liquid (60%) and solid (4%) wastes, and respiration (16%). The moisture in the foods we eat and the water and other fluids we drink replace about 90 percent of this loss. The other 10 percent is generated through metabolic reactions within the body cells.[2]

Recommended water intake varies with age, gender, and activity level. The Food and Nutrition Board of the Institute of Medicine has issued Dietary Reference Intakes (DRI) for water and electrolytes. According to their information, children between four and eight years of age should be getting 1.7 liters (about 7 cups) of water a day. Boys from ages nine to 13 should get 2.4 liters (about 10 cups), and girls in the same age range should get 2.1 liters (about 9 cups). Not all of this intake needs to come from drinking water. All beverages as well as food are sources of this water.

A 10 percent loss of body water brings about major health risks, and a 20 percent loss may result in death.[3] The body can go without water for only a few days, but can live without food for weeks.

1. Solomon, Eldra, Schmidt, Richard R., and Adragna, Peter. *Human Anatomy and Physiology*. Holt, Rinehart and Winston, Inc. New York. 1990.
2. Bevan, James. *Anatomy and Physiology*. Simon and Schuster. New York. 1978.
3. Garrison, Robert H. and Somer, Elizabeth. *The Nutrition Desk Reference*. Keats Publishing, Inc. New Canaan, CT. 1985.

Management

1. Either ask the permission of an average-sized student to be weighed or use an appropriate figure from the *Weight for Age* table. This activity is dependent on data recorded in kilograms. If you are weighing in pounds, use the conversion chart to find kilograms.

Weight for Age: 50th Percentile
(to nearest ½ kg or lb)

Age	Gender	Kilograms	Pounds
8	girls	26	57
	boys	25.5	56
9	girls	29	64
	boys	28.5	63
10	girls	33	72.5
	boys	32	70
11	girls	37	82
	boys	36	79
12	girls	42	92
	boys	40.5	89

Source: National Center for Health Statistics, May 2000

Weight/Mass Conversion Chart
(lbs/2.206, rounded to nearest kg)

Kilograms	Pounds	Kilograms	Pounds
22	48, 49	34	74-76
23	50, 51	35	77, 78
24	52-54	36	79, 80
25	55, 56	37	81, 82
26	57, 58	38	83, 84
27	59, 60	39	85-87
28	61, 62	40	88, 89
29	63-65	41	90, 91
30	66, 67	42	92, 93
31	68, 69	43	94, 95
32	70, 71	44	96-98
33	72, 73	45	99,100

2. Collect empty two-liter bottles. To figure how many you need, divide the number of kilograms in your average student by two.
3. Set the two-liter bottles and liter measuring containers where students will measure and pour the water—either at a sink or in an appropriate outdoor area. Put a funnel in the two-liter bottle being filled to minimize spills.
4. Students should use the same color key for the two-liter bottles, percent graph, and the rice model.
5. To color rice, pour about ¼ cup rubbing alcohol and several drops of food coloring in a jar with a lid. Add the rice and shake to coat. Spread the rice on multiple layers of newspaper to dry. For 30 students, you will need about one cup of rice to represent water and about ¾ cup to represent the rest of the body.

Procedure
Part One

1. Ask the *Key Question* and distribute the first activity page.
2. Find the mass of a student or use data from the *Weight for Age* table in *Management*. Have students record the mass and the equivalent number of liters.
3. Instruct students to find or help them find the amount of water in the body (total liters x .6). Ask how they can find the amount that is not water (total liters x .4). Students should record both computations and round to the nearest deciliter (tenth of a liter or 100 mL).
4. Have students share their results in small groups and resolve differing answers.

Part Two

1. Have students gather at the designated water-pouring area. Let different students take turns measuring a liter of water and pouring it into a two-liter bottle until the amount of water that was calculated has been poured.

2. Students should also assemble the number of empty two-liter bottles that represent the part of the body that is not water. One bottle will likely be part water and part not water.

24 kg: 14.4 L water, 9.6 L not water

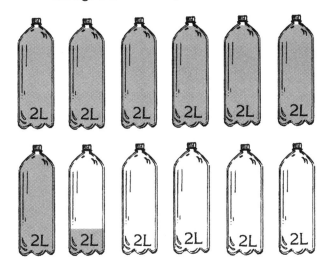

3. After students return to their seats, distribute the second activity page.
4. Have students color the two-liter bottles to represent the total number of bottles (water and *not* water) that are in front of them. The same color key will be used on the third activity page.
5. Tell students to cut along the dashed line, cut out the colored two-liter bottles only, and glue them on the top half of the paper.

Part Three
1. Distribute the third activity page. Explain that the percent graph is divided into 10% segments. Have students use a straight edge to draw lines showing the 60:40 ratio and color these areas using the key from the previous page.
2. Give each student about ½ tablespoon of the rice representing water and about 1 teaspoon of the other color. Demonstrate how to put the smaller amount of rice in the 40% area. Students should fill the area with a single layer and put any leftover rice aside. (They are really doing a form of measuring to show a ratio.)
3. Have students fill the 60% space with the other color of rice in the same way. Circulate and collect any leftover rice.
4. Instruct students to mix the two colors of rice they measured and glue them on the upper circle. This shows that water is dispersed throughout the body, although it is in higher concentrations in some tissues and lower concentrations in others.
5. Give students some background about the water in their bodies and how it relates to their health. Conduct a class discussion.

6. Have students reflect on their learning by responding to the questions on the activity page.

Connecting Learning
1. Where in your body do you think there is water? (See *Background Information*.)
2. Why do people have different amounts of water in their body? [The amount of water depends on age and amount of fat.]
3. How does the body lose water? [sweat, elimination of wastes, respiration (breathe on glass or in cold air to show moisture)]
4. What kinds of activities would cause you to lose greater than average amounts of water? [strenuous work, exercise/sports]
5. Why is it important to replace the water your body loses? [The body needs water to digest food, control its temperature, and carry nutrients and waste products.]
6. How can you replace water your body loses? [There are three sources for replenishing our water supply: water and other fluids (about 60%), food (about 30%), and metabolism (about 10%). School-age children should get between seven and 10 cups of water a day, depending on age and gender.]
7. What are you wondering now?

Extensions
1. Have students monitor and evaluate the amount of water and other fluids they consume in one day. Caution: one glass of soda, fruit juice, tea, or coffee is not necessarily equal to one glass of water. Sugar, caffeine, and alcohol can change the fluid balance.
2. Explore the water content in different foods by doing *Cut and Dried*, another activity in this book.

OUR BODY OF WATER

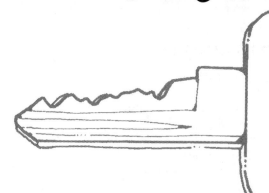

Key Question

How much of your body is water?

Learning Goals

Students will:

- learn how much water is in their bodies, and

- learn the importance of water in maintaining health.

OUR BODY OF WATER

One kilogram of body mass is about equal to one liter of water. The human body is about 60% or $^3/_5$ water.

kg	=	liters	

Mass of person

About how many liters of water does this person have?

How many liters are **not** water?

OUR BODY OF WATER
BY THE LITER

KEY

water   not water

Cut, glue, and color the number of two-liter bottles used to represent the person. Color the key.

2L 2L 2L 2L 2L

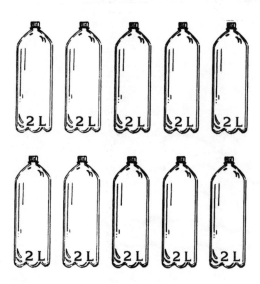

2L 2L 2L 2L 2L

2L 2L 2L 2L 2L

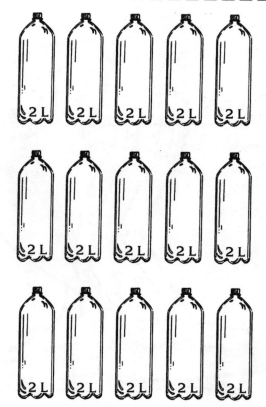

2L 2L 2L 2L 2L

2L 2L 2L 2L 2L

OUR BODY OF WATER

Draw in lines to show the ratio of water to no water in the body. Color the sections using the same colors you used before.

Percent graph

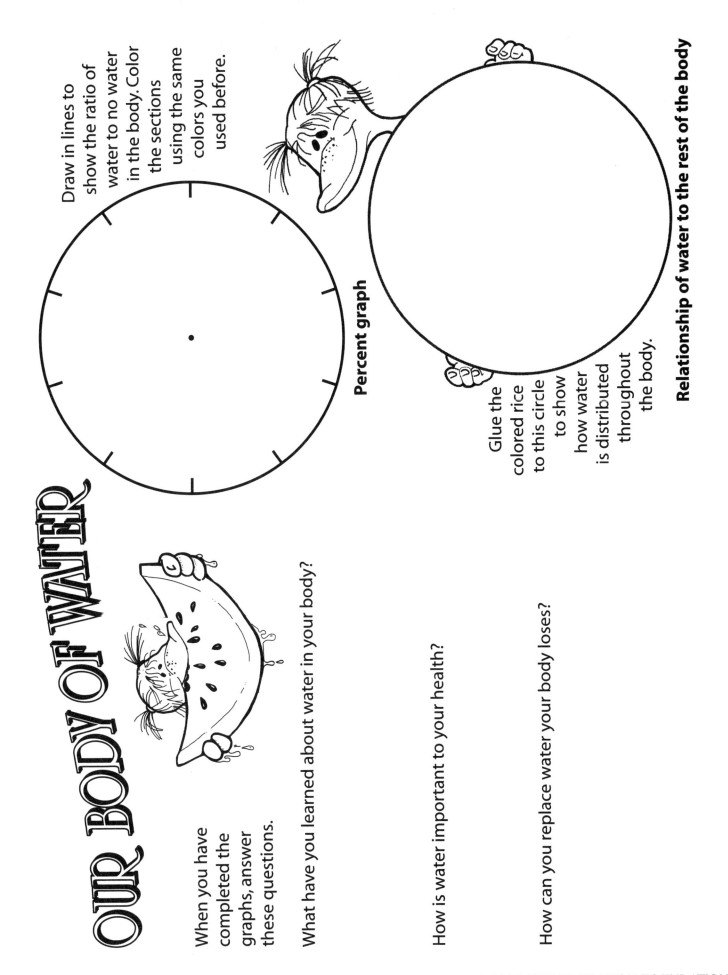

Glue the colored rice to this circle to show how water is distributed throughout the body.

Relationship of water to the rest of the body

When you have completed the graphs, answer these questions.

What have you learned about water in your body?

How is water important to your health?

How can you replace water your body loses?

OUR BODY OF WATER

Connecting Learning

1. Where in your body do you think there is water?

2. Why do people have different amounts of water in their body?

3. How does the body lose water?

4. What kinds of activities would cause you to lose greater than average amounts of water?

5. Why is it important to replace the water your body loses?

6. How can you replace water your body loses?

7. What are you wondering now?

Say AH!

Topic
Teeth

Key Question
How does the number of teeth in your group compare?

Learning Goal
Students will learn about the number and kinds of teeth they have.

Guiding Documents
Project 2061 Benchmarks
- *Spreading data out on a number line helps to see what the extremes are, where they pile up, and where the gaps are. A summary of data includes where the middle is and how much spread is around it.*
- *Geometric figures, number sequences, graphs, diagrams, sketches, number lines, maps, and stories can be used to represent objects, events, and processes in the real world, although such representations can never be exact in every detail.*

NRC Standard
- *Each plant or animal has different structures that serve different functions in growth, survival, and reproduction. For example, humans have distinct body structures for walking, holding, seeing, and talking.*

NCTM Standards 2000*
- *Collect data using observations, surveys, and experiments*
- *Represent data using tables and graphs such as line plots, bar graphs, and line graphs*
- *Solve problems that arise in mathematics and in other contexts*

Math
Counting
Whole number operations
Averages
Graphs

Science
Life science
  human body

Integrated Processes
Estimating
Observing
Classifying
Collecting and recording data
Generalizing

Materials
Mirrors for each student pair
Class graph
Colored paper squares

Background Information
Most mammals grow two sets of teeth. In humans, all of the baby or deciduous teeth generally appear between six months and two years of age. Starting around the age of six or seven, permanent teeth begin to replace the deciduous teeth and continue to emerge until about 21 years of age. Children between the ages of six and 12 will have a combination of baby and permanent teeth. The number and kinds are shown below.

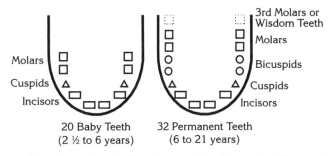

The three basic functions of teeth are to bite and chew, to aid in speaking, and to support facial muscles. Incisors cut like scissors, cuspids cut and shred, bicuspids tear and grind, and molars crush and grind.

Management
1. Student pairs will count each other's teeth, but groups of four or six will pool their data.
2. This activity will take about 60 minutes.

3. Prepare the class graph to record each student's total number of teeth. Refrain from displaying the numbered graph until after predictions have been made. Cut paper squares for students to glue onto the graph.

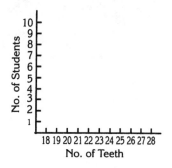

4. Averages will often have remainders. These can be expressed as a remainder, fraction, or rounded number.

$$\overset{22r^2}{4\overline{\smash{)}90}} \text{ or } 22\,^2/_4 \text{ or } 23$$

Procedure

1. Ask the *Key Question* and distribute the activity page.
2. Have students estimate their total number of teeth.
3. Emphasize counting accurately. It is less confusing if teeth are counted by looking at the sides rather than the chewing surface. If the tooth shows above the gum, it is to be counted.
4. Have partners count upper and lower teeth. Instruct them to trade partners and recheck the count. Mirrors may be used.
5. Give each student a paper square and have them glue it above their individual total on the class graph.
6. Students should collect and record data from the rest of their group.
7. Have students find totals and averages for upper, lower, and total teeth. Aid them with finding averages, if needed.
8. Discuss the kinds and functions of teeth. Have them use mirrors to make a pictorial record of their teeth on the activity sheet. Using the key, give guidance in drawing teeth and leaving spaces where they are missing.

Connecting Learning

1. What was the least number of teeth in our class? the most number of teeth? (range)
2. What is the most common number of teeth in our class? (mode average)
3. Do you think the results would be about the same in other classes? Why or why not? [The number of teeth will vary with age, developmental rates, and dental needs. Humans have fewer baby teeth than permanent teeth and may not have a full set of permanent teeth until about 21 years of age.] Make a hypothesis and devise a plan for testing it.
4. Do you think we did an accurate job of counting? Why or why not?
5. What are you wondering now?

Extensions

1. Obtain x-rays from a dentist. Put them on the overhead projector and have students compare the structures of the different kinds of teeth. If available, compare x-rays of baby teeth to those of adult teeth.
2. Find the class' average number of teeth. Use individual totals rather than group averages.
3. Gather data from a different age group and compare results.

Curriculum Correlation

Language Arts

1. Read the book *How Many Teeth?* by Paul Showers (HarperCollins, 1991). Through written for a young audience, it traces how the number of teeth change from babyhood to adulthood.
2. Have students write a story or diary from a tooth's point of view.

Social Science

Have students research George Washington's teeth (thought to be wooden but actually ivory).

Health

1. Tie this activity to National Dental Health Month (February) and discuss tooth care (brushing, flossing, and dental visits).
2. Ask the school nurse to bring in a model of teeth.
3. Have students draw and label the different layers of a tooth.

* Reprinted with permission from *Principles and Standards for School Mathematics*, 2000 by the National Council of Teachers of Mathematics. All rights reserved.

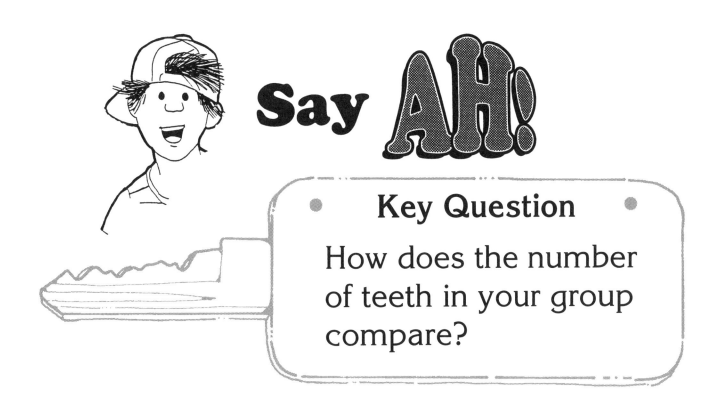

Say AH!

Key Question

How does the number of teeth in your group compare?

Learning Goal

Students will:

learn about the number and kinds of teeth they have.

Say AH!

Your Total Teeth

Estimate: _____

Actual: _____

Name	Upper Teeth	Lower Teeth	Total Teeth
Totals			
Averages			

How does the number of teeth in your group compare?

Draw your teeth.

Incisors	▭
Cuspids	△
Bicuspids	○
Molars	▢

UPPER

LOWER

Say AH!

Connecting Learning

1. What was the least number of teeth in our class? ...the most number of teeth?

2. What is the most common number of teeth in our class?

3. Do you think the results would be about the same in other classes? Why or why not? Make a hypothesis and devise a plan for testing it.

4. Do you think we did an accurate job of counting? Why or why not?

5. What are you wondering now?

I've Got Rhythm

Topic
Heart rate

Key Question
How does exercise affect your heartbeat?

Learning Goal
Students will explore how their heart rate relates to various exercises.

Guiding Documents
Project 2061 Benchmark
- *There are normal ranges for body measurements—including temperature, heart rate, and what is in the blood and urine—that help to tell when people are well. Tools, such as thermometers and x-ray machines, provide us clues about what is happening inside the body.*

NRC Standard
- *Regular exercise is important to the maintenance and improvement of health. The benefits of physical fitness include maintaining healthy weight, having energy and strength for routine activities, good muscle tone, bone strength, strong heart/lung systems, and improved mental health. Personal exercise, especially developing cardiovascular endurance, is the foundation of physical fitness.*

NCTM Standards 2000*
- *Collect data using observations, surveys, and experiments*
- *Represent data using tables and graphs such as line plots, bar graphs, and line graphs*
- *Solve problems that arise in mathematics and in other contexts*

Math
Counting
Whole number operations
Graphs

Science
Life science
   human body

Integrated Processes
Observing
Predicting
Collecting and recording data
Comparing
Generalizing
Applying

Materials
Clock/watch with second hand
Transparency of graph, optional

Background Information
Heart rates vary with age, sex, size, environment, temperature, and other factors. The normal heart rate for adults is 60 to 80 beats per minute. Children's heart rates are faster. According to biological data, newborns average 134 beats per minute with a range between 100 and 180, six to eight year olds average 100 beats (70-115), and nine to 11 year olds average 88 beats (60-110).

It is estimated the heart beats three billion times by age 70, about 42 million beats per year. The average human body has about 5.7 liters (about six quarts) of blood. Each beat moves only about 59 milliliters (more than two fluid ounces) of blood out into the arteries, so the blood must circulate rapidly to meet the needs of the body.

The goal during aerobic exercise is to keep the heart pumping at 130 to 150 beats per minute for a sustained period of time, usually 20 or more minutes. This strengthens the heart and keeps blood vessels in good working condition. One desirable and likely effect of long-term aerobic conditioning is a lower resting heart rate.

Management
1. This activity will take about 45 to 60 minutes.
2. Decide the time length to be used for counting heartbeats: 20 seconds (x 3), 15 seconds (x 4), or 10 seconds (x 6). Multiply by the amount indicated to find heartbeats per minute.
3. Students are responsible for taking their own pulse rates. They should press their index and middle fingers against the inside of the wrist or on one side of the neck. The thumb should not be used because it can have a pulse of its own.

(The following approach is offered for those teachers whose students are ready for more independent investigations.)

> *Open-ended:* Ask the *Key Question.* Have students design and carry out a plan to answer it. They should report their results.

Procedure
1. Ask the *Key Question.* After receiving responses, give students the activity page.

2. Have students predict and record their resting pulses. They should also record the time length during which they will count their heartbeats.
3. Time students as they count their resting heartbeats. Have them compute their resting rate per minute in the space provided.
4. Allow one to two minutes of brisk walking, preferably outdoors, before students count and compute their walking pulse. As the students are getting ready to count their pulses after walking or running, have them feel for their pulse *before* they actually stop so they will be ready to start counting immediately when the signal is given. Use the following hints to obtain accurate results:
   a. Have the students silently mouth their counting instead of just thinking it; counting out loud is confusing.
   b. Take more than one reading of each activity as some will not have counted correctly. Screen their answers by having each one quickly say their count. A general guide:

	15 seconds	60 seconds
Resting	12-25	50-100
Walking	22-38	90-150
Running	40-55	160-220

5. Have students run for one to two minutes, count, and compute their running pulse.
6. Provide time for students to complete the graph, study it, and write about the results.
7. Guide a class discussion.

Connecting Learning
1. What would happen if you tried to count one full minute? [heartbeat would slow and change results, might lose count]
2. What did you discover?
3. Why is exercise good for your heart? [Your heart is a muscle and needs to stay in good condition.]
4. What kinds of exercise would strengthen your heart? [fast walking, running, swimming, skipping rope, cycling, dancing, soccer, basketball, etc.]
5. What are you wondering now?

Extensions
1. Find the class range for each activity (lowest-highest).
2. Find the average heart rate for each activity.
3. Combine this activity with a study of the circulatory system. Your school nurse may be able to obtain a pig's or cow's heart from the butcher to show the structure of the heart.

Curriculum Correlation
Physical Education
Experiment with aerobic exercise and see if it lowers your heartbeat over a period of time.

Language Arts
Find words and expressions that use *heart* and discuss their meanings.

heartache	heart to heart
heartbroken	to one's heart's content
heartburn	get to the heart of
heartfelt	eat one's heart out
heartstring	to wear one's heart on
heartless	one's sleeve
heart-throb	heavy heart
heart-warming	

Home Link
Encourage students to compare the resting pulses of members of their family.

* Reprinted with permission from *Principles and Standards for School Mathematics*, 2000 by the National Council of Teachers of Mathematics. All rights reserved.

I've Got Rhythm

Key Question

How does exercise affect your heartbeat?

Learning Goal

explore how their heart rate relates to various exercises.

I've Got Rhythm

How does exercise affect your heartbeat?

I predict my resting pulse is _____.

Count your pulse for _____ seconds.

Multiply by _____ to find the number of heartbeats per minute.

RESTING   WALKING   RUNNING

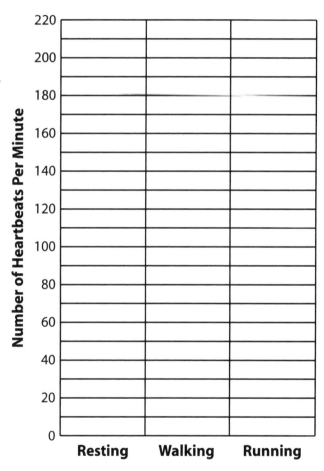

Number of Heartbeats Per Minute

220
200
180
160
140
120
100
80
60
40
20
0

Resting   Walking   Running

What did you discover?

I've Got Rhythm

Connecting Learning

1. What would happen if you tried to count one full minute?

2. What did you discover?

3. Why is exercise good for your heart?

4. What kinds of exercise would strengthen your heart?

5. What are you wondering now?

Topic
Opposable thumbs

Key Question
How important are your thumbs?

Learning Goals
Students will:
- learn about the unique qualities of the human hand, and
- see how its design affects the way they live.

Guiding Documents
Project 2061 Benchmarks
- *Measuring instruments can be used to gather accurate information for making scientific comparisons of objects and events and for designing and constructing things that will work properly.*
- *Use numerical data in describing and comparing objects and events.*

NRC Standard
- *Each plant or animal has different structures that serve different functions in growth, survival, and reproduction. For example, humans have distinct body structures for walking, holding, seeing, and talking.*

NCTM Standards 2000*
- *Collect data using observations, surveys, and experiments*
- *Represent data using tables and graphs such as line plots, bar graphs, and line graphs*
- *Select and apply appropriate standard units and tools to measure length, area, volume, weight, time, temperature, and the size of angles*
- *Solve problems that arise in mathematics and in other contexts*

Math
Measurement
   time
Whole number operations
Averages
   mean, mode
Estimation
   rounding
Graphs

Science
Life science
   human body

Integrated Processes
Observing
Collecting and recording data
Comparing and contrasting
Controlling variables
Generalizing

Materials
Stopwatch
Class graph (see *Management 7*)

(The following materials are for the activities suggested in *Management*. You may plan your own activities with supplies that are readily available to you.)

Zippered pants
Shirt with buttons
Combs
Cereal
Sugar
Milk
Bowls
Spoons
Crackers
Peanut butter
Table knife
Sandwich bags
Books
Pencil activity
Ball
Phone
Scissors activity
Chart paper

Background Information
   Hands are designed for taking hold of objects. Human hands have opposable thumbs—thumbs that can be moved against the fingers. Our thumbs make it possible for us to grip things and make delicate movements. Human progress would have been greatly changed by the absence of opposable thumbs.

   The parts of the human hand are the wrist, the palm, the four fingers, and the thumb. There are twenty-seven bones in the hand; eight in the wrist, five in the palm, three in each finger and two in the thumb.

The hand is moved by 35 muscles. Fifteen muscles are in the forearm, giving the hand great strength. Near the wrist, the muscles become tendons that run along the palm and the back of the hand to the fingers.

Management

1. *Thumb Fun* takes about one week and can be run concurrent with regular classroom activities. The suggested activities take eight to 20 minutes per student, per race.
2. Set up stations with activities that simulate daily tasks and involve as much gripping as possible. Some suggested activities are:
   - GETTING UP: Start race in a reclining position, shoes off.
   - DRESSING: Use a slightly baggy shirt and pants that students can slip over their school clothes.
   - FIX AND EAT BREAKFAST: Provide cereal, spoons, bowls, milk, and sugar. Students are to fix and eat a mini-breakfast.
   - MAKE LUNCH: Provide crackers and peanut butter to make a sandwich. Have students place it in a bag and take it with them.
   - GO TO SCHOOL: Students go to another part of the room carrying their lunch and a stack of books.
   - SCHOOL WORK (pencil): Use an activity that is difficult but does not have so much writing as to become frustrating. Math drills work well.
   - RECESS: Activities that involve gripping a ball are good to use. Students could throw a foam ball into a wastebasket.
   - PHONE HOME: Students dial home on a disconnected phone.
   - SCHOOL WORK (scissors): Make a simple pattern for the students to cut out.
   - EAT LUNCH: Students are to eat the sandwich they prepared earlier.
   - GO HOME: If available, have the students (while carrying their stack of books) open and close a door with a door knob.
   - UNDRESS: Students remove shoes and baggy shirt and pants.
   - GO TO BED: Students return to reclining position. The race is over.
3. The activities are performed twice, first with the use of thumbs and then with the thumbs taped. Thumbs should be taped across or next to the palms of the hands.
4. Races should be run exactly alike both times. The only variable to change is the use of thumbs. Be very specific in deciding how each activity will be performed.
5. Students in groups of three or four can take turns as runners, timers, and recorder/guides.

6. Start timing with the beginning of the first activity and stop timing with the completion of the final activity. Times should be rounded to the nearest minute. If a student is not able to complete an activity, he/she is to keep trying for 30 seconds, after which a 60-second penalty is added to his/her time.
7. Make a class graph on chart paper for recording the difference between thumbs and thumbless times for each student. Have students place small sticky note above the numbers indicating their times.

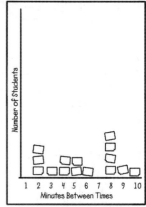

Procedure

1. Have the class brainstorm daily activities that involve using hands. Guide them in deciding which of those activities could be acted out in the classroom.
2. Distribute the first page and have students list the chosen activities in the order in which they will be performed. Involve students in collecting materials.
3. Form groups, set up the race, and have volunteers model how each activity is to be done. Emphasize that the data collected will have value only if the activities are done the same way each time by everyone. This is called controlling variables.
4. Supervise the initial races. While one group member operates the timer, another should use the activity page to check off each activity as it is completed or record the penalty time if not completed. Times should be rounded to the nearest minute.
5. Subsequent races can be run, a few each day, until everyone has had a turn. Have students complete the graph at the bottom of the page.
6. Distribute the group data page. Have students collect and record data from the other group members.
7. Instruct students to find the group's average time difference and show their computation on the page.
8. Have students construct a graph of the average time difference and write their conclusions.
9. Supervise as students complete the class graph. Use this graph as well as their other data for a class discussion.

Connecting Learning

1. Which race was the most difficult?
2. What kinds of activities were hard to do without the use of your thumbs? [Activities that involve gripping will be the most difficult.] Why were these activities difficult?
3. How do your own times compare with those in your group? ...with those in your class?

4. Look at the class graph. What is the range of time differences for our class? (lowest difference to highest difference) Which time difference was the most common for our class? (mode)
5. What did you learn from this activity?
6. What do you appreciate about your thumbs?

Extensions
1. Have students read about monkeys/chimpanzees, focusing on thumbs.
2. Have students read about the hands of other animals and how they are adapted to different types of activities.

Curriculum Correlation
Language Arts
1. Make a list of *thumb* and *hand* compound words.
2. Discuss idiomatic expressions using *thumb* and *hand* such as "all thumbs, thumbs down, give a hand, hand in," etc.
3. Write "Thumb Twisters." Example: Thadeus Thornthort, Thane of Thebes, thumbed the thesaurus thankfully.
4. Write a story about how the world would be different if everyone were thumbless.

Social Science
The human hand helps people to communicate with each other as in the sign language of the North American Indian. Study Indian sign language.

Physical Education
1. Play a favorite game thumbless.
2. Invent a new thumbless game.

Art
1. Have students sculpt or draw their hands.
2. Trace around both hands and decorate the drawing. Write sentence strips, "These hands like to ...." Hand tracings can also be used to make turkeys, reindeer antlers, wreaths, etc.
3. Art appreciation can be taught with emphasis upon the hand as it appears in art work. In addition to being the central focus of a piece, the hand may also be used in gesture to complete a line, to highlight an area, or to set a mood. *The Creation of Adam* by Michelangelo, copied by Steven Spielberg in E.T. (Did E.T. have opposable thumbs?) is an excellent example of the use of the hand in art.

* Reprinted with permission from *Principles and Standards for School Mathematics*, 2000 by the National Council of Teachers of Mathematics. All rights reserved.

THUMB FUN

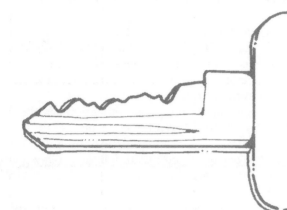

Key Question

How important are your thumbs?

Learning Goals

Students will:

- learn about the unique qualities of the human hand, and

- see how its design affects the way they live.

THUMB FUN

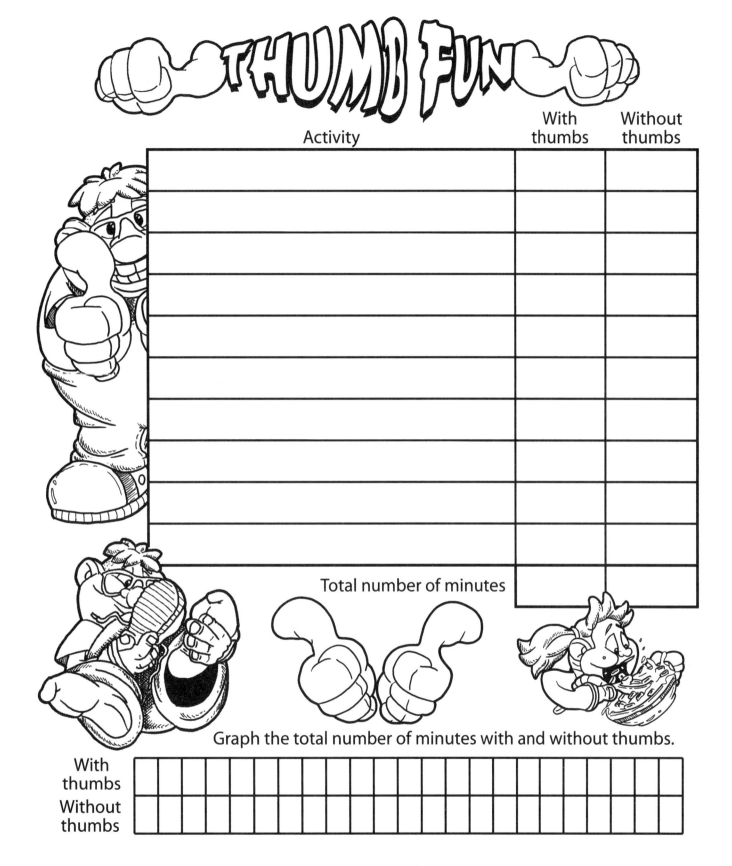

Activity	With thumbs	Without thumbs
Total number of minutes		

Graph the total number of minutes with and without thumbs.

With thumbs																							
Without thumbs																							

Number of minutes

How important are your thumbs?

Group Data

Name				
Total minutes with thumbs				
Total minutes without thumbs				
Difference in time				

Find and graph the average time difference for your group.

Your conclusion:

Connecting Learning

1. Which race was the most difficult?

2. What kinds of activities were hard to do without the use of your thumbs? Why were these activities difficult?

3. How do your own times compare with those in your group? ...with those in your class?

4. Look at the class graph. What is the range of time differences for our class? Which time difference was the most common for our class?

5. What did you learn from this activity?

6. What do you appreciate about your thumbs?

Gimme Five!

Topic
Fingerprints

Key Question
How do our fingerprints compare?

Learning Goals
Students will:
- observe and classify their fingerprints,
- use a bar graph to examine class data, and
- draw conclusions about the results.

Guiding Documents
Project 2061 Benchmarks
- *Features used for grouping depend on the purpose of the grouping.*
- *Some likenesses between children and parents, such as eye color in human beings, or fruit or flower color in plants, are inherited. Other likenesses, such as people's table manners or carpentry skills, are learned.*
- *Graphical display of numbers may make it possible to spot patterns that are not otherwise obvious, such as comparative size and trends.*

NRC Standards
- *Tools help scientists make better observations, measurements, and equipment for investigation. They help scientist see, measure, and do things that they could not otherwise see, measure and do.*
- *Employ simple equipment and tools to gather data and extend the senses.*

NCTM Standards 2000*
- *Collect data using observations, surveys, and experiments*
- *Represent data using tables and graphs such as line plots, bar graphs, and line graphs*

Math
Patterns
Data analysis
    graphing

Science
Life science
    human body

Integrated Processes
Observing
Classifying
Collecting and recording data
Comparing and contrasting
Generalizing
Applying

Materials
For each student:
    soft-leaded pencil
    7 pieces of transparent tape, about 1.5" long
    3" x 3" paper for pencil rubbing
    2" x 2" yellow paper for class graph
    hand lens

For the class:
    class graph (see *Management 1*)
    glue

Background Information
Scientists look for patterns in what they observe. They develop hypotheses as possible explanations for the way things are.

Most fingertips have patterns of ridges separated by valleys. In the valleys, there are small holes. Each of these holes is a small pore through which sweat or moisture oozes from the gland within. The ridge pattern is the fingerprint and is slightly different from any other fingerprint in the world. Three basic types (loop, arch, and whorl) are pictured and described in *Basic Fingerprint Patterns*. See the *Fingerprinting* fact sheet for further information.

Management
1. Prepare a three-column class graph labeled *Loop, Arch,* and *Whorl*. This particular order spells *LAW*, an easy way to remember the types of prints.
2. It is helpful to make a transparency of *Basic Fingerprint Patterns*.
3. Suggestions for handling the tape:
    a. Give each group a tape dispenser and have them tear off their own pieces.
    b. Put a "starter set" of three or so pieces on the edge of each desk while students are at recess. Then circulate and add more pieces as they do the activity.
4. Make sure students use the pad of their finger (the area just above the top joint) for their fingerprints, not the tip.
5. Usually students can clean their fingers with a tissue.
6. This activity will take about 40 minutes.

Procedure

1. Ask the *Key Question*.
2. Use *Basic Fingerprint Patterns* to explain the types of prints.
3. Distribute transparent tape, the 3" x 3" square of paper, and soft-leaded pencils.
4. Have students rub the pencil lead on the small square of paper. This accumulation of graphite forms the "ink pad."
5. Direct students to trace or draw the outline of one of their hands on the activity page.
6. Have students rub one finger at a time on the graphite pad, transfer the print by placing a strip of transparent tape along the length of the finger pad, and gently lifting it from the finger. Have them place the print on the corresponding finger of the hand drawing. Direct them to do each digit the same way.
7. Proved hand lenses for students to analyze the types of fingerprints. Encourage them to record the type by printing L for *Loop,* A for *Arch,* and W for *Whorl* by each print.
8. Have each student compare the types of fingerprints on his/her hand.
9. As a class, choose one finger to be represented on the large class graph. Have students make another print of this finger, tape it on the 2" x 2" yellow paper, and glue the paper in the correct column on the class graph.
10. Guide the reporting of class data for each finger and have students graph the data to determine the most common types.
11. Compare like types for individual differences.
12. Have students make an extra copy of one of the fingerprints and tape it in the cookie jar on the activity page.
13. Direct students to trade papers and match the cookie jar print to one of the five fingerprints on the hand tracing.

Connecting Learning

1. Which type of fingerprint is most common? Which is least common?
2. Are the fingerprints the same on all your fingers? Are the fingerprint patterns the same on your right hand and your left hand? Explain.
3. Predict the left index fingerprint of your teacher. Why did your predict this?
4. Why do you think the police department records all 10 of your fingerprints?
5. How are fingerprints valuable?
6. What are you wondering now?

Extensions

1. As students are doing *Gimme Five!,* circulate around the room and ask each student to make an extra print of his or her right index finger and put it on a small piece of yellow paper. All samples should be placed in the same direction on the paper. Do not tell students for what this will be used. On a large piece of chart paper, place the fingerprint samples in six rows. Put a line under each sample and write "Please sign in:" at the top. Keep the chart up for several days, if needed, until everyone has found his or her own print and signed the chart.

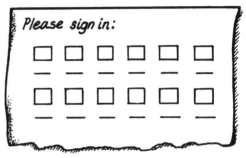

2. Make a "Mystery Print" bulletin board by gathering sets of teachers' fingerprints plus extras for the mystery print. Have students find the matching print.
3. Explore one of these questions:
   Do girls' prints differ from boys'?
   Do ethnic groups have certain print patterns?
   Are toeprints like fingerprints?
   Are fingerprints hereditary?
   Can you get rid of your fingerprints? Do they regenerate?
   Does my dog have different footprints than another dog?
4. Invite a police investigator to visit and discuss fingerprint classification.

* Reprinted with permission from *Principles and Standards for School Mathematics,* 2000 by the National Council of Teachers of Mathematics. All rights reserved.

Gimme Five!

> ## Key Question
>
> How do our fingerprints compare?

Learning Goals

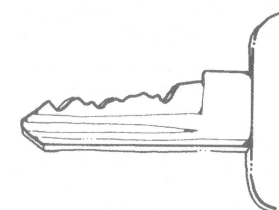

Students will:

- classify their fingerprints,

- use a bar graph to examine class data, and

- draw conclusions about the results.

Fingerprinting

Fingerprinting, the science of using the friction ridge pattern on the fingertips for identification, is one of the earliest forms of scientific evidence to be recognized by courts of law. Its formal name is dactyloscopy. It is now recognized universally as a system of personal identification. These ridges and creases are found on monkeys, apes, gorillas, orangutans, and some kinds of birds as well as humans.

A fingerprint is the impression left upon any surface with which the finger comes in contact under pressure. There are also toeprints, palm prints, soleprints (footprints), and lip prints.

The history of fingerprinting goes back as far as prehistoric carvings found on cliffs in Nova Scotia and on the walls of a Neolithic burial site off the coast of France. Since the second century B.C., the Chinese have used finger impressions for sealing documents. In 1823 the first dissertation was written on the subject, and in 1893 Sir Frances Galton proved that no two prints were alike. The following year the first identification of a criminal was made based on his fingerprints.

The Henry system of identication includes eight types of patterns that are shown here. (For additional details, writings by Sir Frances Galton and Juan Vucetich are helpful.) Contrary to popular belief, the ridges of the fingerprints are lined with moisture or sweat, not oil, that causes a print to be made. Twins, triplets, and quadruplets all have completely different prints. Latent prints can be dusted and lifted for up to several months after the impression is made and up to 10 years later if laser technology is used. A fingerprint cannot be forged or counterfeited. The FBI has nearly 200 million fingerprints on file. It identifies over 2700 fugitives a month through fingerprints.

Fingerprints are divided for identification into eight types of patterns, known as the Henry system.

1. Plain arch

2. Tented arch

3. Radial loop

4. Ulnar loop

5. Plain whorl

6. Central packet loop

7. Double loop

8. Accidental

BASIC FINGERPRINT PATTERNS

LOOP

Loops have lines entering at one side of the finger pad and leaving on the same side.

ARCHES

Arches have lines entering on one side of the finger pad and leaving on the opposite side.

WHORL

Whorls have lines entering at the side of the finger pad and spiraling inward, ending in the center.

Gimme Five!

Draw an outline of your hand.
Transfer a fingerprint to each finger.

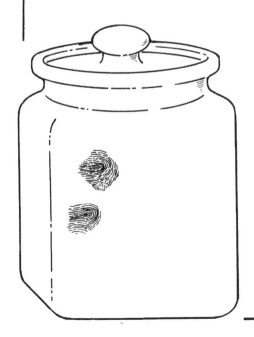

**Who put the cookies
in the cookie jar?**

Gimme Five!

Little

	Loop	Arch	Whorl
20			
19			
18			
17			
16			
15			
14			
13			
12			
11			
10			
9			
8			
7			
6			
5			
4			
3			
2			
1			
0			

Ring

	Loop	Arch	Whorl
20			
19			
18			
17			
16			
15			
14			
13			
12			
11			
10			
9			
8			
7			
6			
5			
4			
3			
2			
1			
0			

Middle

	Loop	Arch	Whorl
20			
19			
18			
17			
16			
15			
14			
13			
12			
11			
10			
9			
8			
7			
6			
5			
4			
3			
2			
1			
0			

Index

	Loop	Arch	Whorl
20			
19			
18			
17			
16			
15			
14			
13			
12			
11			
10			
9			
8			
7			
6			
5			
4			
3			
2			
1			
0			

Thumb

	Loop	Arch	Whorl
20			
19			
18			
17			
16			
15			
14			
13			
12			
11			
10			
9			
8			
7			
6			
5			
4			
3			
2			
1			
0			

Gimme Five!

Connecting Learning

1. Which type of fingerprint is most common? Which is least common?

2. Are the fingerprints the same on all your fingers? Are the fingerprint patterns the same on your right hand and your left hand? Explain.

3. Predict the left index fingerprint of your teacher. Why did you predict this?

4. Why do you think the police department records all 10 of your fingerprints?

5. How are fingerprints valuable?

6. What are you wondering now?

Flexible Feet

Topic
Human body: feet

Key Question
Why should you stand up when trying on new shoes?

Learning Goal
Students will find that their feet spread, particularly in length, when they stand.

Guiding Documents
Project 2061 Benchmarks
- *Things change in steady, repetitive, or irregular ways—or sometimes in more than one way at the same time. Often the best way to tell which kinds of change are happening is to make a table or graph of measurements.*
- *Areas of irregular shapes can be found by dividing them into squares and triangles.*
- *Use numerical data in describing and comparing objects and events.*

NRC Standards
- *Each plant or animal has different structures that serve different functions in growth, survival, and reproduction. For example, humans have distinct body structures for walking, holding, seeing, and talking.*
- *Employ simple equipment and tools to gather data and extend the senses.*

NCTM Standards 2000*
- *Select and apply appropriate standard units and tools to measure length, area, volume, weight, time, temperature, and the size of angles*
- *Represent data using tables and graphs such as line plots, bar graphs, and line graphs*

Math
Estimation
Measurement
    length
    area
Whole number operations

Science
Life science
    human body

Integrated Processes
Observing
Collecting and recording data
Comparing and contrasting
Generalizing
Applying

Materials
Metric rulers
2 colored pencils for each student pair

Background Information
The human foot is composed of 26 bones. Tough cords called tendons connect the bones to muscles. Over 100 ligaments, which are strong, flexible bands, connect the bones to each other. The bones, tendons, and ligaments help a person move. They also support the body's mass in a balanced, upright position. The short bones are mainly associated with support and the five long bones (metatarsals) with movement. Skin provides a protective covering that is about 5 mm thick on the soles of the feet.

It is estimated the average person will walk or run about 110,000 km (68,000 miles) during a life-time—nearly three times around the world. With each step, the tendons stretch, the space between the bones increases, and the foot flattens. When the foot is lifted, the tendons retract, and the bones move closer together.

Some suggest that the best time to shop for shoes is late afternoon or evening, when feet have flattened the most after being walked on all day. Because feet spread when force is exerted on them, it is important to test the fit of new shoes by standing and walking.

Shoe size does not necessarily determine if shoes will fit. Different companies use different lasts—foot-like forms on which shoes are made. Each successive American shoe size is generally ⅓" longer and each half size ⅙" longer, but other foot measurements used in making the lasts may cause the fit to vary. (European sizes and lasts are different yet.) Between the ages of four and 11, the feet grow about ⅓" or one shoe size a year.

Management
1. Pairs of students should work together.
2. A smooth, hard surface is needed to make the foot tracings. Students will need to remove one shoe

and sock for the tracings. Inform them of this the day before so they will be prepared.

3. Students should find several ways to compare their two foot tracings. Among these might be measuring length, width, and area. Area is most easily figured by counting any square where half or more is inside the tracing as a whole square centimeter. Students could mark each square that counts with a dot or in some other way.

Procedure

1. Ask the *Key Question* and gather responses. Distribute the grid paper, activity page, and colored pencils.
2. Instruct one student of each student pair to stand with feet slightly apart, one foot on the grid paper, directly in front of a chair. Tell the partners to trace around their feet, keeping the colored pencil nearly vertical or perpendicular to the floor.
3. Have the students being traced sit in the chairs without moving their feet. Instruct the partners to use the second different colored pencil to trace their feet again.
4. Ask partners to trade places and repeat steps two and three.
5. Encourage partners to discuss ways to compare their standing foot and sitting foot. They should conduct the comparisons, then organize and record the results inside the foot on the activity page.
6. Have students make a general statement of their results at the bottom of the paper.
7. Hold a class discussion, after which students can answer the second question on the page.

Connecting Learning

1. What did you notice by looking at the tracings? Why do you think this is so? (Listen to their thoughts, then use *Background Information* to complement or clarify their thinking.)
2. Are your results what you expected?
3. Were the results consistent throughout the class? What might cause differences? [putting most of the body mass on the foot not being traced, position of pencil when tracing, etc.]
4. How can the results be useful to you? [test the fit of shoes by standing in them with a better understanding of why this is important] What shoe-fitting experiences have you had that would support what we discovered today?
5. What are you wondering now?

Extension

Have students carry out a plan to answer one of the following questions or one of their own:

a. When comparing sitting and standing feet, does age make a difference?
b. Does size of feet make a difference?
c. Do people with feet of the same size wear shoes of the same size?

Home Link

Students could trace the feet of the members of their families and compile the results.

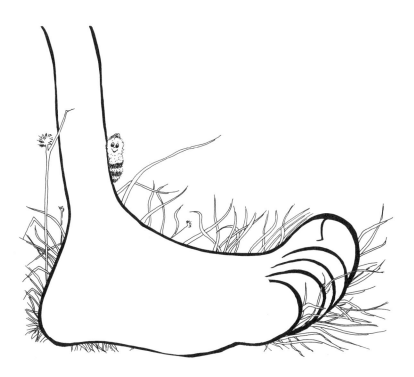

Flexible Feet

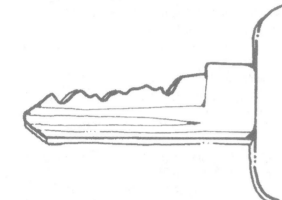

Key Question

Why should you stand up when trying on new shoes?

Learning Goal

Students will:

find that their feet spread, particularly in length, when they stand.

Flexible Feet

Why should you stand up when trying on new shoes?

Stand and have your partner trace around your foot on the grid paper. Without lifting your foot, sit down and have your partner trace again using a different color.

Compare your "sitting foot" with your "standing foot" in several ways. Record below.

What were your results?

How do your results compare with others?

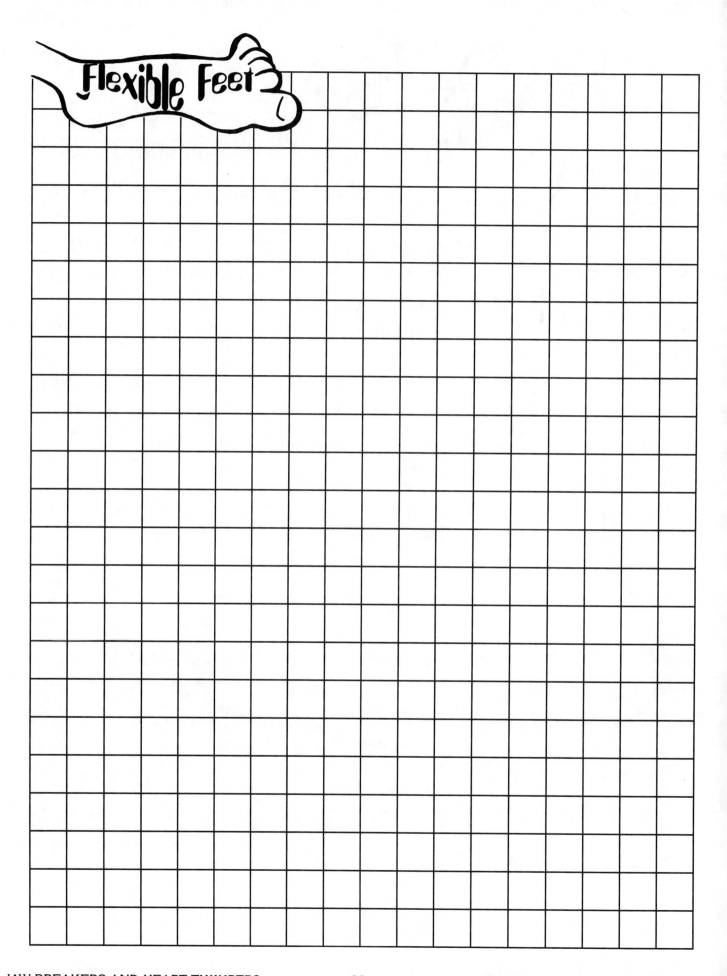

Flexible Feet

Flexible Feet

Connecting Learning

1. What did you notice by looking at the tracings? Why do you think this is so?

2. Are your results what you expected?

3. Were the results consistent through-out the class? What might cause differences?

4. How can the results be useful to you? What shoe-fitting experiences have you had that would support what we discovered today?

5. What are you wondering now?

compression session

Topic
Human body: spine

Key Question
How does your height change during the day?

Learning Goal
Students will measure and compare their morning heights with their afternoon heights.

Guiding Documents
Project 2061 Benchmarks
- *Measuring instruments can be used to gather accurate information for making scientific comparisons of objects and events and for designing and constructing things that will work properly.*
- *Recognize when comparisons might not be fair because some conditions are not kept the same.*

NRC Standards
- *Each plant or animal has different structures that serve different functions in growth, survival, and reproduction. For example, humans have distinct body structures for walking, holding, seeing, and talking.*
- *Employ simple equipment and tools to gather data and extend the senses.*

NCTM Standards 2000*
- *Collect data using observations, surveys, and experiments*
- *Represent data using tables and graphs such as line plots, bar graphs, and line graphs*
- *Select and apply appropriate standard units and tools to measure length, area, volume, weight, time, temperature, and the size of angles*
- *Solve problems that arise in mathematics and in other contexts*

Math
Measurement
    length
Whole number operations
Decimals

Averages
Graphs

Science
Life science
    human body

Integrated Processes
Predicting
Observing
Identifying and controlling variables
Collecting and recording data
Comparing and contrasting
Generalizing

Materials
Meter sticks

Background Information
The spine provides support and flexibility and protects the spinal cord from injury and disease. It is composed of separate bones called vertebrae. Sandwiched between the vertebrae are soft cartilage discs that act as cushions. Gravity and daytime activity squeeze some of the fluid out of the discs, making the backbone slightly shorter. During the night, the spongy discs expand as fluid again accumulates. For this reason, a person is a little shorter (about a half centimeter or so) in the evening than in the morning but recovers his or her height during sleep.

Management
1. Decide whether measures will be done to the nearest half centimeter (.5) or the nearest millimeter. The millimeter measure provides more accurate results.
2. This activity takes one week to complete, about 10 minutes per day. A longer time will be needed on the introductory and culminating days.
3. Students will need instruction in measuring height accurately. The first-day measurement might be done by the teacher to obtain an accurate guide.
4. Decide the two times measurements will be taken, one in the morning and one in the afternoon. The greater the span of time between the two measurements, the better.

(The following approaches are offered for those teachers whose students are ready for more independent investigations.)

> *Open-ended:* Ask small groups of students to devise a plan for testing the *Key Question*. Making a prediction, assuring accuracy, repeated trials, and a graphics display should be evidenced in their planning and results.
>
> *Guided planning:* Give each small group the *Plan Sheet* as a framework to help them organize their investigation of the *Key Question*. Give guidance where needed.

Procedure

1. Ask the *Key Question* and give students the first activity page.
2. Brainstorm possible predictions as a whole class and have students write their choices on the page. The three possibilities are: you get taller, you get shorter, or you stay the same.
3. Discuss together how to make accurate measurements (see *Connecting Learning*) and stress their importance.
4. On the first day, measure each student in the morning and again in the afternoon. Have them record the times and results.
5. Guide students, if needed, in calculating their height change. Have them show their computations in the space below the table.
6. On succeeding days, student groups can do their own measuring and find the amount of change. After five days, have students complete the discovery statement.
7. Give students the average/graph page and help them find their average amount of change. One way is by using one students' results and going through the process on the overhead projector.
8. Divide students into groups of five and have them record the averages of each member to complete the graph.
9. Hold a class discussion and have students write a statement about the results.

Connecting Learning

1. How will you make sure measurements will be done the same way each time? [shoes should be taken off, person needs to stand straight, the rigid tool placed on the head and against the height measure needs to be parallel to the floor]
2. How did your height change?
3. Who stayed the same height all day long? Who shrank the most?
4. Did you shrink the same amount each day?
5. What do you think makes you get smaller? (see *Background Information*)

6. If you had a choice, what time of the day would you want to be measured for school health records? Why?
7. What do you think happens to the height of an astronaut in a gravity-free environment?
8. How fast do you think your spine compresses? Does it compress at the same rate all day long or is it completely compressed in an hour or two? Make a plan to investigate these questions.

Extensions

1. Have students gather data on the effects of various activities such as sitting, running, hanging on the bars, etc., have on shrinkage. Or they might compare active with non-active days.
2. Students could explore the effect of fluid intake on shrinkage.

Curriculum Correlation

Health

Students can study about injuries to the spinal column and the handicaps such injuries can cause. A study of safety rules would be appropriate at this time.

Art

Groups of students could make a clay model of the spinal column.

Home Link

1. Have students ask their parents if they have to adjust the rear view mirror when they drive home from work in the afternoon. How might this relate to this activity?
2. Suggest that students measure family members. Does the amount of height change differ with age?

* Reprinted with permission from *Principles and Standards for School Mathematics,* 2000 by the National Council of Teachers of Mathematics. All rights reserved.

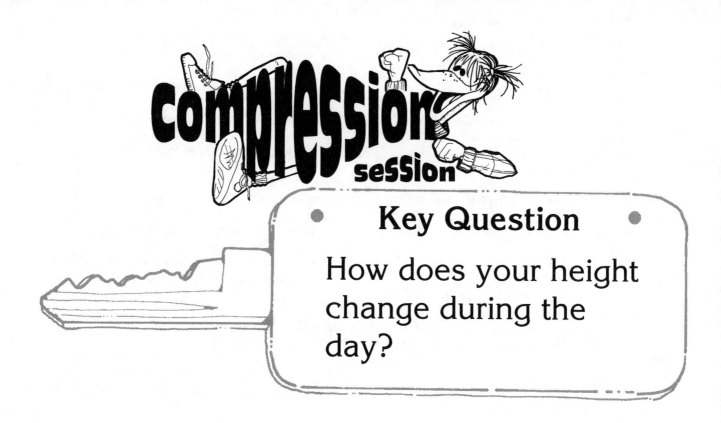

Key Question

How does your height change during the day?

Learning Goal

Students will:

measure and compare their morning heights with their afternoon heights.

How does your height change during the day?

compression
session
Plan Sheet

1. What are the possible predictions? Put an X by your prediction.

2. Who will be measured?

3. How will you make sure measurements are done the same way each time?

4. At what times and for how many days will measuring be done?

5. Sketch how you plan to record the results.

6. After completing your investigation, what new questions do you have?

compression
session

How does your height change during the day?

My prediction:

How will you make sure measurements are done the same way each time?

Time	Height (nearest _____)				
	Mon.	Tues.	Wed.	Thurs.	Fri.
_____					
_____					
Change	_____	_____	_____	_____	_____

Find your height change each day.

I discovered that:

Transfer your height changes from the first page.

Find your average change, if any, for the week.

Monday _____ cm

Tuesday _____ cm

Wednesday _____ cm

Thursday _____ cm

Friday _____ cm

Circle your results:

grew

stayed the same

shrank

What statement can you make about the results?

Average Height Change

6				
5.5				
5				
4.5				
4				
3.5				
3				
2.5				
2				
1.5				
1				
.5				
0				

Centimeters

_____ _____ _____ _____ _____
Group Members

Connecting Learning

1. How will you make sure measurements will be done the same way each time?

2. How did your height change?

3. Who stayed the same height all day long? Who shrank the most?

4. Did you shrink the same amount each day?

5. What do you think makes you get smaller?

6. If you had a choice, what time of the day would you want to be measured for school health records? Why?

7. What do you think happens to the height of an astronaut in a gravity-free environment?

8. How fast do you think your spine compresses? Does it compress at the same rate all day long or is it completely compressed in an hour or two?

ABOUT TIME FOR FOOD

Topic
Importance of breakfast

Key Question
Why do you need breakfast?

Learning Goals
Students will:
• keep a record of the times they eat, and
• consider the importance of breakfast in contributing to good physical and emotional health.

Guiding Documents
Project 2061 Benchmarks
• *Food provides energy and materials for growth and repair of body parts. Vitamins and minerals, present in small amounts in foods, are essential to keep everything working well. As people grow up, the amounts and kinds of food and exercise needed by the body may change.*
• *Physical health can affect people's emotional well-being and vice versa.*

NRC Standard
• *Nutrition is essential to health. Students should understand how the body uses food and how various foods contribute to health. Recommendations for good nutrition include eating a variety of foods, eating less sugar, and eating less fat.*

NCTM Standards 2000*
• *Collect data using observations, surveys, and experiments*
• *Select and apply appropriate standard units and tools to measure length, area, volume, weight, time, temperature, and the size of angles*
• *Solve problems that arise in mathematics and in other contexts*

Math
Measurement
    time
Estimation
    rounding
Graph
    circle

Science
Life science
    health and nutrition

Integrated Processes
Observing
Collecting and recording data
Comparing and contrasting
Applying

Materials
Clock
Crayons or colored pencils
Straight edge
Transparency of activity page

Background Information
The nutrients in food provide energy for people to perform their daily activities. While most people eat periodically during the day, there is a lengthy interval of time between dinner (or evening snack) and the next meal. During this time, the body uses up most of its supply of protein, carbohydrates, and other nutrients which provide energy. Blood glucose (sugar) levels are low.

The brain is the body's primary user of blood glucose. While a child's brain is as big as an adult's, a child's liver, where glucose is stored, is much smaller; it can only hold about a four-hour supply. For the brain to function adequately, an average child 10 years or younger needs to eat fairly often.

Eating very little or nothing for a prolonged period of time such as overnight is called a *fast*. Breakfast literally means to *break a fast*, to refuel the body. If the body's energy supply is not replenished, continued low levels of blood glucose will affect a person physically, emotionally, and in the performance of tasks. Headaches, stomach cramps, lack of energy, and malnutrition are some of the potential physical effects. Emotionally, the lack of food tends to cause irritability. An inadequate supply of blood glucose to the brain makes it difficult to concentrate on work.

With no fuel, it is hard to work or learn. Breakfast provides nutrients so a person can be alert and work more productively. In recognition of the importance of breakfast, the United States government funds a low-cost breakfast program reaching more than 7.4 million children at over 72,000 sites each school day.

Management

1. Since data will be gathered for a 24-hour period and then analyzed, this activity will take a class session on each of two consecutive days.
2. Consider recording from lunch one day to lunch the next day since these will be common eating times for the whole class.
3. Allow ample time for students to study the graph and write statements. It is important that they learn to interpret data.
4. The graph shows 24 hours. Each hour is divided into 10-minute segments. Students should round times to the nearest 10 minutes.
5. Be sensitive to situations where families are struggling to provide meals.

Procedure

1. Ask the *Key Question*: "Why do you need breakfast?" Record responses on a transparency or chart paper.
2. Distribute the activity page. Have students read the directions and set up a way to record the necessary data. You may wish to have the class start by recording lunch data.
3. Discuss what is considered eating. Drinking water does not count, but drinking a soda or eating any kind of food does.
4. Instruct students to take the paper home, record every time they eat even a little bit, and return with the paper the next day.
5. The next day, demonstrate how to make the graph. Have them use a straight edge to draw the lines.
6. Instruct students to label each line they draw as *breakfast, lunch, dinner,* or *snack* and fill each section with a different color.
7. Have students calculate the longest time, in hours and minutes, their bodies went without food.
8. On the back or on another sheet of paper, have students write several statements that can be made from studying their graph. They may also write questions that can be answered from the graph.
9. Ask students to share some of their statements. Discuss the results together and give them further information on the importance of breakfast.

Connecting Learning

1. Based on your graph, what statements can you make?
2. How is your daytime eating different from your nighttime eating? [You generally eat more often during the day and less at night.] Why? [You are sleeping during the night.]
3. Why is food important to people? [It gives us energy, helps us grow, etc.]
4. What is in food that helps us be healthy? (Elicit student responses about what they already know about food nutrients such as vitamins, minerals, protein, carbohydrates, etc.)
5. How does lack of food affect you? [You might be grumpy, get mad easily, be tired, have difficulty concentrating or thinking, have a malnutrition problem, etc. It affects you both physically and emotionally.]
6. Why do some people skip breakfast? [lack of time, don't like breakfast-type food, etc.] How could this problem be solved? [choose foods that don't take much time to make, eat healthy foods you like (you aren't limited to breakfast foods), etc.]

Extensions

1. Students can calculate the number of hours and minutes for each section in the circle graph.
2. Save the students' papers and repeat this activity on another day. Have them compare their eating habits on the two days.

Curriculum Correlation

Literature

Burns, Marilyn. *Good For Me!* Little Brown and Company. Boston. 1978.
(Chapter 26 is entitled, "Is Breakfast Really So Important?")

Fritz, Jean. *George Washington's Breakfast.* Putnam & Grossett Group. New York. 1998.
(The main character tries to find out what George Washington ate for breakfast.)

Sharmat, Mitchell. *Gregory, the Terrible Eater.* Scholastic, Inc. New York. 1980.
(A light-hearted tale built around a goat who tries new foods, many at breakfast.)

Social Science

1. Research what people in other countries eat for breakfast or what was eaten in other centuries.
2. Not all people in the world have enough food available to them. They may not be able to choose if they have breakfast or not. Identify some of these places and think about reasons for the lack of food (drought, poor soil for growing crops, not enough money to buy food, etc.) Discuss efforts that have been made to help those in need.

* Reprinted with permission from *Principles and Standards for School Mathematics*, 2000 by the National Council of Teachers of Mathematics. All rights reserved.

ABOUT TIME FOR FOOD

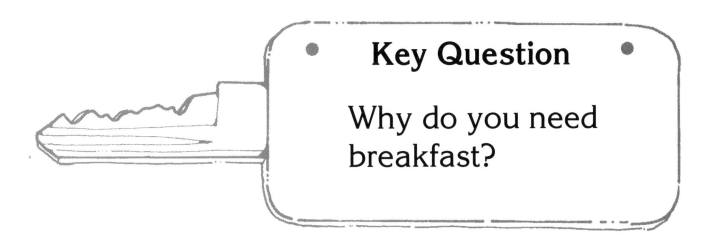

Key Question

Why do you need breakfast?

Learning Goals

Students will:

- keep a record of the times they eat, and

- consider the importance of breakfast in contributing to good physical and emotional health.

ABOUT TIME FOR FOOD

Why do you need breakfast?

Each time you eat today, record the time and whether it is breakfast, lunch, dinner, or a snack.

Mark the times you ate, drawing a line to the center dot. Use a different color to fill the space between each set of lines.

24-hour Graph

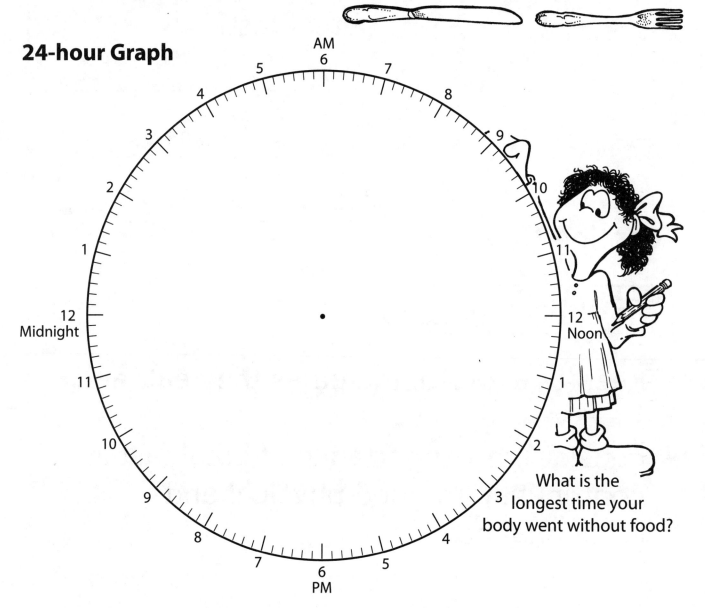

What is the longest time your body went without food?

78

ABOUT TIME FOR FOOD

Connecting Learning

1. Based on your graph, what statements can you make?

2. How is your daytime eating different from your nighttime eating? Why?

3. Why is food important to people?

4. What is in food that helps us be healthy?

5. How does lack of food affect you?

6. Why do some people skip break-fast? How could this problem be solved?

PYRAMID of Choices

Topic
USDA's MyPyramid

Key Question
How can the foods in this grocery bag be sorted?

Learning Goal
Students will learn to classify foods according to the groups represented on the USDA's MyPyramid.

Guiding Documents
Project 2061 Benchmark
• *Food provides energy and materials for growth and repair of body parts. Vitamins and minerals, present in small amounts in foods, are essential to keep everything working well. As people grow up, the amounts and kinds of food and exercise needed by the body may change.*

NRC Standard
• *Nutrition is essential to health. Students should understand how the body uses food and how various foods contribute to health. Recommendations for good nutrition include eating a variety of foods, eating less sugar, and eating less fat.*

Math
Sorting

Science
Life science
    health and nutrition

Integrated Processes
Observing
Classifying
Comparing and contrasting
Applying

Materials
For each student:
    1 piece of 12" x 18" construction paper, any color
    1 set of pyramid sections, included
    food picture cards (see *Management 4*)
    1 piece of 6" x 18" white construction paper
    1 set of response cards in six colors (see *Management 5*)
    scissors

colored pencils
glue stick

For the class:
    grocery bag filled with assorted foods or food containers
    food pictures from magazines, grocery ads, or food labels
    6 pieces of chart paper
    colored copy paper (see *Management 3*)
    envelopes, 1 for every two students
    tape
    Internet access
    large food pyramid for bulletin board, optional

Background Information
The original USDA Food Guide Pyramid was first introduced in 1991, then modified and released in final form in 1992. In 2005, a revised food guide called My-Pyramid was released. This revised pyramid looks very different from the 1992 version, and emphasizes the importance of determining your individual diet needs based on gender, age, and physical activity level.

The categories in the revised MyPyramid are grains, vegetables, fruits, milk, meat and beans, and oils. Discretionary calories are also included, which encompass fats, added sugars, and alcohol. Physical activity is now an integral part of the pyramid. Instead of listing the recommended number of servings per day, the new pyramid gives actual amounts, in cups or ounces, that should be consumed each day.

The largest section of MyPyramid is grains. Grains provide the *carbohydrates* needed for energy. Grains include any products made from wheat, rice, oats, cornmeal, or other cereal grains. The current recommendation is for at least half of the grains consumed to be whole, rather than refined. This includes whole wheat bread, oatmeal, and brown rice. Refined grains, while often enriched with vitamins, contain none of the fiber in whole grains, and are more quickly processed by your body, leading to spikes in blood sugar.

The vegetable and fruit groups both supply the *vitamins* needed for everything from healthy skin, bones, nerves, and blood to cell processes. Vitamin A is prominent in vegetables, vitamin C in fruits. Variety is important in both fruit and vegetable intake, and limiting your intake of fruit juices (which are high in sugar) is advisable.

The body uses *minerals* for the growth and maintenance of body structures. Calcium, obtained from the milk group, strengthens the bones and teeth. It is important to select low-fat or fat-free milk products whenever possible. Also avoid foods with added sugars, like some flavored yogurts.

About three-fourths of the solid parts of the body such as muscles, hair, bones, teeth, and the brain are made of protein. *Protein*, provided by the meat and beans group, is necessary to build and repair these parts. Again, lean and low-fat choices are the wisest, and fish, beans, peas, nuts, and seeds are recommended.

As in the original pyramid, oils (more a category than a food group) are to be used sparingly. Trans fats are to be avoided completely, and saturated fats should be limited. Most oils should come from fish, nuts, and vegetable oils. These oils do not contain saturated fat, and will not raise the level of bad (LDL) cholesterol in the blood.

In addition to the food guidelines, MyPyramid recommends finding a balance between food intake and physical activity. Being physically active for at least 30 minutes each day is important to maintaining health.

Management

1. This activity is divided into two parts. *Part One* introduces the food groups as defined by the new USDA recommendations. It can be done over the course of a week or more to allow one day to introduce each of the sections of the pyramid. *Part Two* can be used as an assessment after students have explored each of the sections.
2. Collect foods or food containers and food pictures. Consider adding cultural foods representative of your school population.
3. Copy each page of pyramid sections onto the appropriate color of paper. You will need orange, green, red, yellow, blue, and purple paper.
4. Duplicate the food pictures sheets on card stock. Laminate and cut apart, making one set for every two students. These will be the students' food picture sorting cards.
5. Prepare the following pieces of construction paper for each student:
   a. Cut 6" x 2.5" pieces of orange, green, red, yellow, blue, and purple so each student has one of each color. These will be the response cards for *Part Two*.
   b. Cut 6" x 18" pieces of white construction paper, one per student.
6. Cut the *Food Group Labels* page in half so each student can be given a set of six.

Procedure

Part One: Introduction to the Food Groups
1. After asking the *Key Question*, let the students sort grocery bag foods in several ways: like/don't like, shapes, colors, etc. Then say, "I have a different way for us to sort. We can put foods together by the special material they have that our bodies need to grow and stay healthy."
2. Introduce the grains group. Brainstorm foods in this group and list them on a piece of chart paper. Have students use the USDA's website to read more about the foods in the grains group (see *Internet Connections*).
3. Distribute the 12" x 18" piece of construction paper and a grains pyramid section to each student. Have them glue the section to the construction paper about 2.5 inches from the left edge so that the bottom of the section is about 1.5 inches from the bottom of the paper.

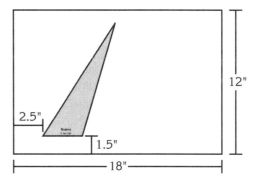

4. Give students colored pencils and have them draw several foods that belong in the grains section.
5. Pair up students and give each pair an envelope containing the set of *Food Picture Sorting Cards*. Have them sort the pictures into two groups: grains and others. Check the groupings through class discussion. Have the students return the cards to the envelopes to save for future use.
6. Distribute the vegetable section of the pyramid and have students glue it just to the right of the grains section.
7. Repeat *Procedures 2-6* of for vegetables.
8. Review the food groups by sorting the food cards into grains, vegetables, and others.
9. Continue this same procedure, adding the fruits, oils, milk, and meats sections until the pyramid is finished.
10. Have students read about discretionary calories on the MyPyramid and discuss why the USDA might have chosen to eliminate sweets from the food pyramid.
11. Have students draw a set of stairs up the left side of the pyramid to represent the physical activity component. Discuss the importance of physical activity to a healthy lifestyle.

12. Optional: Use collected food pictures or labels to fill a large teacher-created bulletin board pyramid as each food group is discussed or after all the food groups have been introduced.

Part Two: Food Group Practice
1. Distribute the colored construction paper pieces and one set of food group labels to each student. Have them glue the labels to the tops of the construction paper pieces using the colors from the pyramid as a guide.
2. Show students how to form card holders by making a two-inch fold along the length of the 6" x 12" white construction paper and taping up the edges.

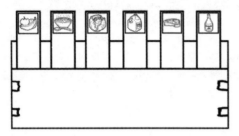

3. As food is taken out of the grocery bag, have students, on signal, hold up the matching response card.

Connecting Learning
1. From what food group should we pick the most foods each day? [grains] What kind of grains should they be? [whole grains]
2. Which food group makes up the smallest portion of the pyramid? [oils] Why? [Oils are high in fat and can have negative health consequences if consumed in large quantities.] Are some oils better than others? [yes] Explain. [Polyunsaturated and monounsaturated oils have fewer calories and do not raise the levels of bad cholesterol in your blood. These oils can be found in fish, nuts, and vegetable oils.]
3. What food groups did you eat for lunch today? Was your meal well-balanced according to the pyramid? Why or why not?
4. Which sections of the pyramid do you need to be getting more of? Which sections should you be eating less of?
5. Where do sugars and sweets fit into the pyramid? [They are part of your discretionary calories—you should only eat them after you've met your other nutritional needs and still have calories left to consume.]
6. Why is physical activity a part of the pyramid?
7. What are you wondering now?

Extensions
1. Go to the MyPyramid website and have students use the Pyramid Tracker to determine how well their diets and activity levels conform to healthy standards.
2. Make food journals by stapling six pieces of paper together. Prepare a set of food pictures on regular paper for each student. Have each student cut out the grains and glue them on the first page of the food journal. Label the food group. Repeat for the other food group pictures.
3. Use the response cards to identify foods from the school lunch menu.

Internet Connections
USDA MyPyramid
http://www.mypyramid.gov/
This website explores the new food pyramid in depth and includes tools for analyzing your diet and activity levels.

Home Link
Give each student a paper plate to draw what he or she ate for dinner that night. The next day have students verbally identify the food groups they drew on the paper plates.

PYRAMID of Choices

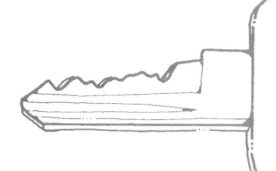

Learning Goal

Students will:

learn to classify foods according to the groups represented on the USDA's MyPyramid.

FOOD GROUPS

Grains
(carbohydrates)

Whole grains:
brown rice
wild rice
oatmeal
popcorn
whole wheat bread
whole wheat crackers
whole wheat pasta
whole wheat sand-
 wich buns and rolls
whole wheat tortillas

Refined grains:
cornbread
tortillas
crackers
grits
noodles
pretzels
corn flakes
white bread
white sandwich buns
 and rolls
white rice

Fruits
(vitamins)

apples
apricots
avocados
bananas
berries
grapefruit
grapes
melons
nectarines
peaches
pears
pineapple
oranges

Vegetables
(vitamins)

Dark green vegetables:
broccoli
collard greens
romaine lettuce
spinach

Orange vegetables:
acorn squash
butternut squash
carrots
pumpkin
sweet potatoes

Starchy vegetables:
corn
green peas
potatoes

Other vegetables:
asparagus
bean sprouts
beets
Brussels sprouts
cabbage
cauliflower
celery
eggplant
green beans
green or red peppers
iceberg (head) lettuce
mushrooms
okra
onions
zucchini

Milk
(calcium)

cheese
cottage cheese
frozen yogurt
ice cream
ice milk
milk
puddings made with milk
yogurt

Meat & Beans
(protein)

almonds
bacon
beef
black beans
cashews
chicken
eggs
fish
ham
hamburger
lamb
peanuts
peanut butter
pecans
pinto beans
pistachios
pork
seafood
split peas
sunflower seeds
turkey
veal
walnuts

Oils
(fat)

Oils:
canola oil
corn oil
cottonseed oil
olive oil
safflower oil
soybean oil
sunflower oil
vegetable oil

Solid fats:
butter
lard
stick margarine
shortening

Foods that are mainly oils:
mayonnaise
salad dressings
tub margarine

PYRAMID
of Choices

Copy onto orange paper. Each student needs one section.

Grains
6 ounces

Grains
6 ounces

PYRAMID of Choices

Copy onto green paper. Each student needs one section.

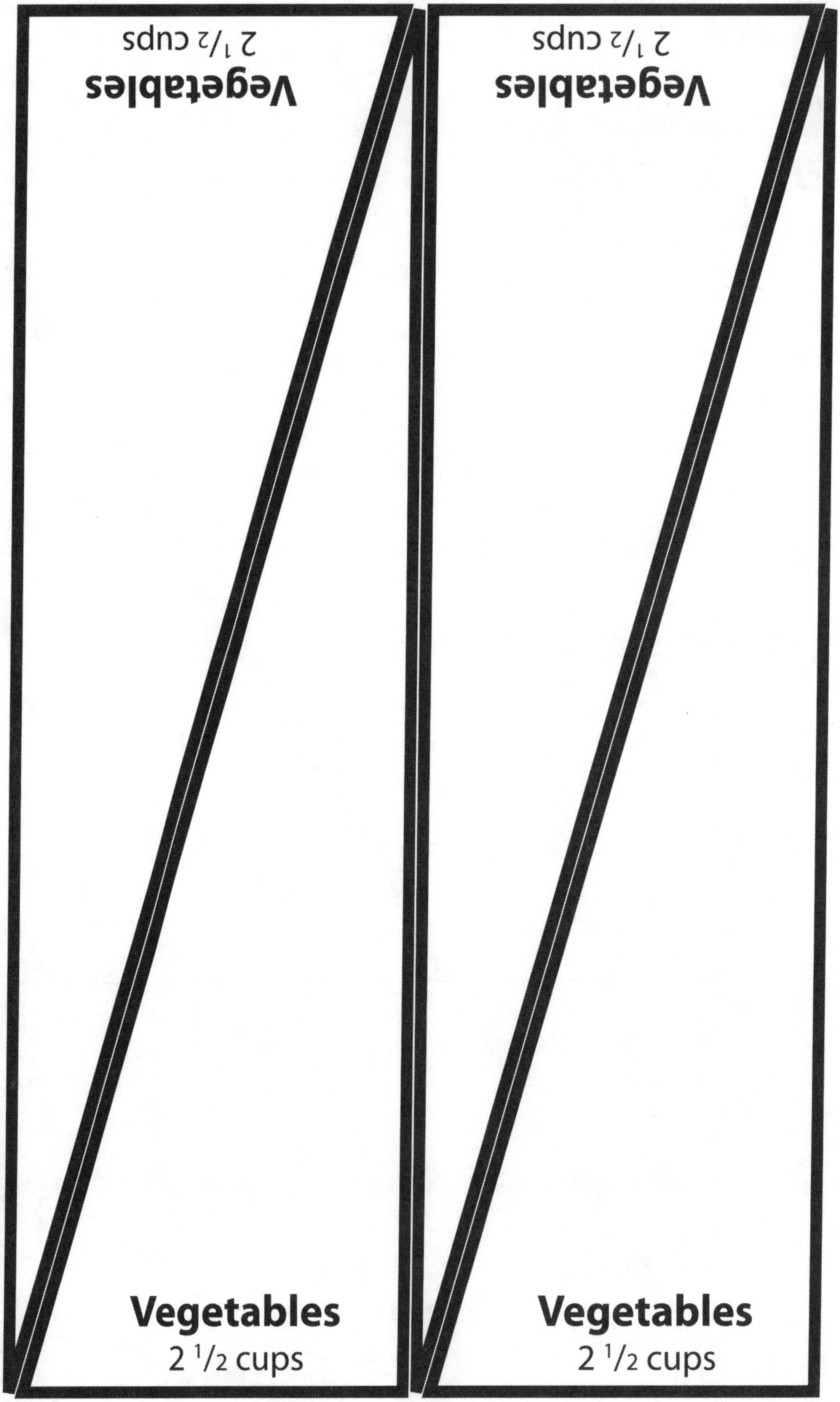

Vegetables
2 ¹/₂ cups

Vegetables
2 ¹/₂ cups

Vegetables
2 ¹/₂ cups

Vegetables
2 ¹/₂ cups

PYRAMID
of choices

Copy onto red paper. Each student needs one section.

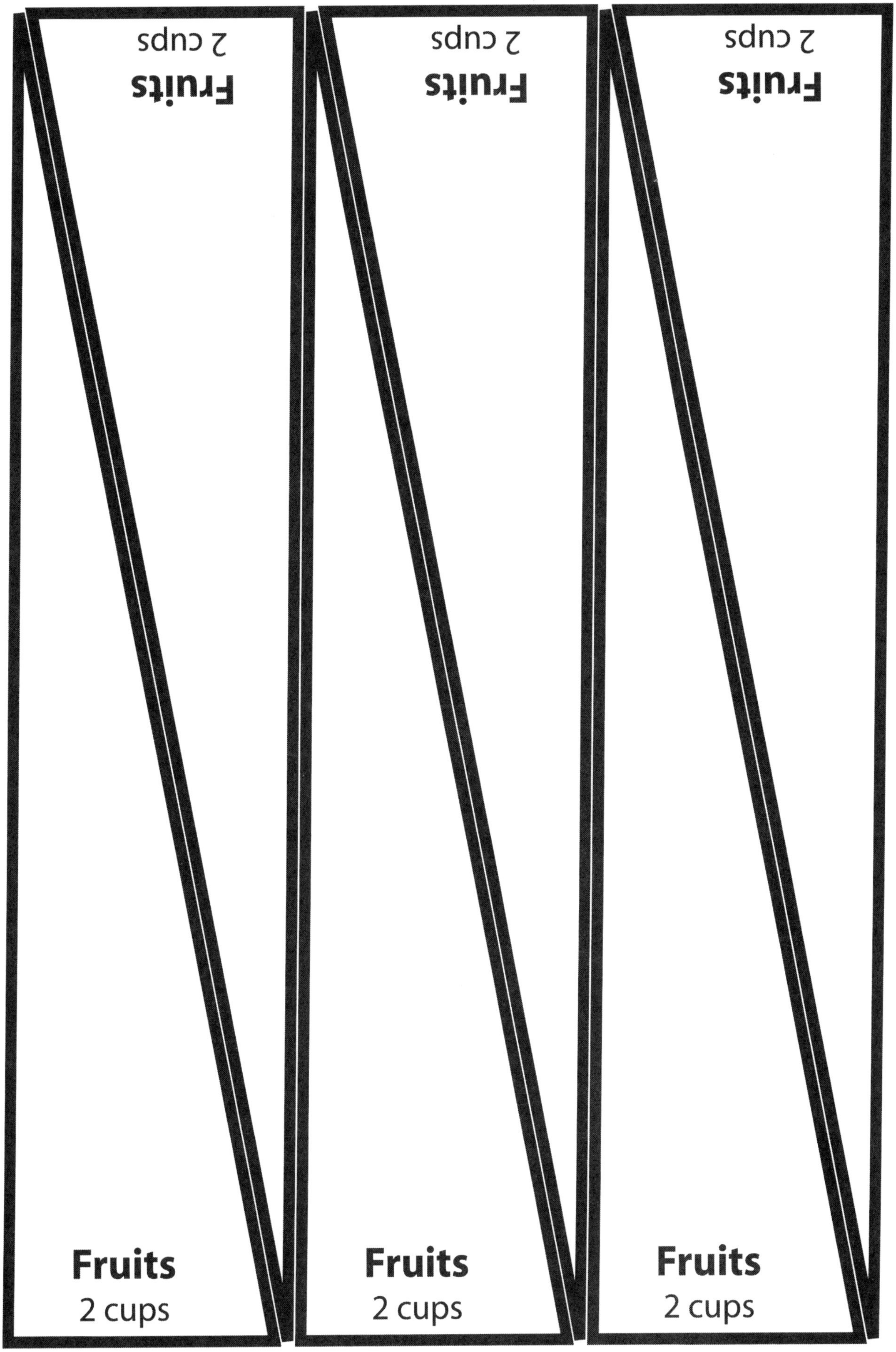

Fruits
2 cups

Fruits
2 cups

Fruits
2 cups

Fruits
2 cups

Fruits
2 cups

Fruits
2 cups

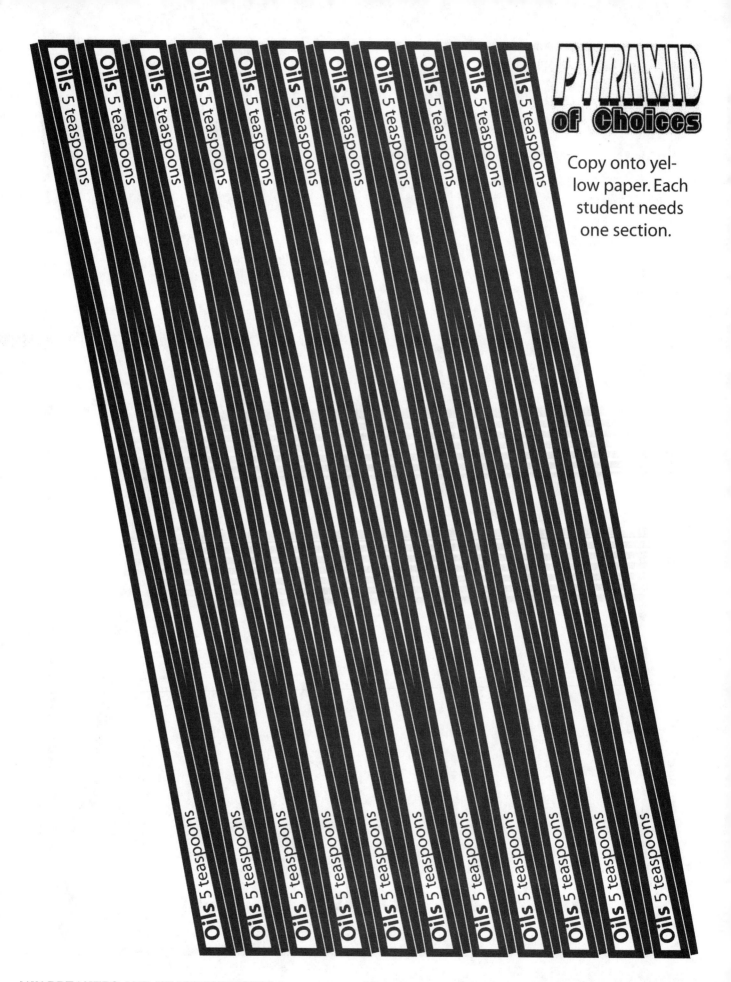

PYRAMID
of Choices

Copy onto yellow paper. Each student needs one section.

Oils 5 teaspoons

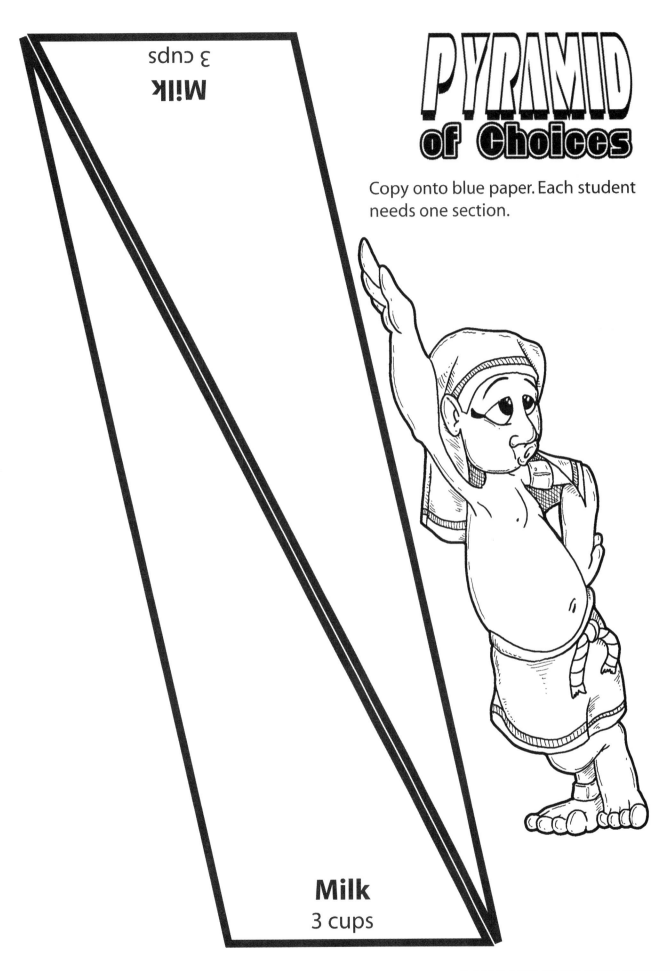

Milk 3 cups

PYRAMID
of Choices

Copy onto blue paper. Each student needs one section.

Milk
3 cups

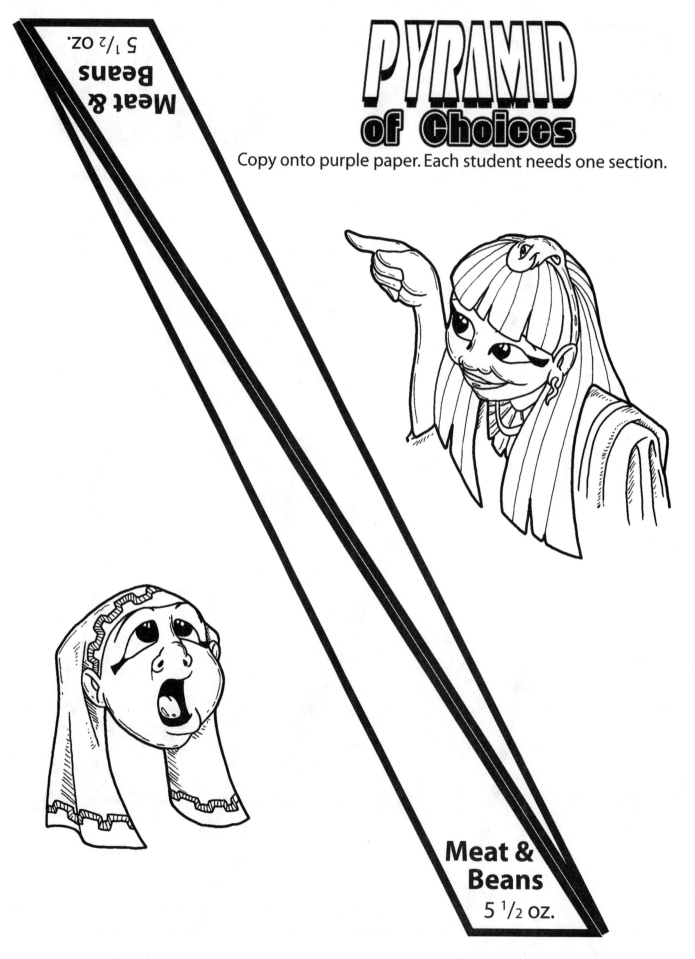

PYRAMID
of Choices

Copy onto purple paper. Each student needs one section.

Meat &
Beans
5 ½ oz.

Meat &
Beans
5 ½ oz.

Food Group Labels

Grains (Orange)	**Vegetables** (Green)	**Fruits** (Red)

"Make half your grains whole"	"Vary your veggies"	"Focus on fruits"
Milk (Blue)	**Meat & Beans** (Purple)	**Oils** (Yellow)
	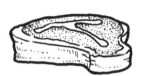	
"Get your calcium-rich foods"	"Go lean with protein"	"Know your fats"
Grains (Orange)	**Vegetables** (Green)	**Fruits** (Red)

"Make half your grains whole"	"Vary your veggies"	"Focus on fruits"
Milk (Blue)	**Meat & Beans** (Purple)	**Oils** (Yellow)

"Get your calcium-rich foods"	"Go lean with protein"	"Know your fats"

apple	bacon	bread
butter	yogurt	avocado
chicken	corn flakes	fish
milk	carrots	olive oil
broccoli	peanuts	muffin
melon	salad dressing	rice

beans

cheese

crackers

bananas

corn

eggs

mayonnaise

cherry pie

lettuce

pasta

strawberries

potato chips

hamburger

almonds

pancakes

cottage cheese

pumpkin

pudding

Connecting Learning

1. From what food group should we pick the most foods each day? What kind of grains should they be?

2. Which food group makes up the smallest portion of the pyramid? Why? Are some oils better than others? Explain.

3. What food groups did you eat for lunch today? Was your meal well-balanced according to the pyramid? Why or why not?

4. Which sections of the pyramid do you need to be getting more of? Which sections should you be eating less of?

5. Where do sugars and sweets fit into the pyramid?

6. Why is physical activity a part of the pyramid?

7. What are you wondering now?

Fat FINDERS

Topic
Fat in food

Key Question
How do the foods you selected compare to each other in terms of fat content?

Learning Goals
Students will:
- use food labels to determine the amount of fat in a meal they have chosen, and
- compare this to the recommended 35% limit of daily calories from fat.

Guiding Documents
Project 2061 Benchmarks
- *Toxic substances, some dietary habits, and personal behavior may be bad for one's health. Some effects show up right away, others may not show up for many years. Avoiding toxic substances, such as tobacco, and changing dietary habits to reduce the intake of such things as animal fat increases the chances of living longer.*
- *Add, subtract, multiply, and divide whole numbers mentally, on paper, and with a calculator.*

NRC Standard
- *Nutrition is essential to health. Students should understand how the body uses food and how various foods contribute to health. Recommendations for good nutrition include eating a variety of foods, eating less sugar, and eating less fat.*

NCTM Standards 2000*
- *Collect data using observations, surveys, and experiments*
- *Represent data using tables and graphs such as line plots, bar graphs, and line graphs*

Math
Whole number operations
Data analysis
 ratios
 decimals
 percents
Estimation
 rounding

Science
Life science
 health and nutrition

Integrated Processes
Observing
Collecting and recording data
Comparing and contrasting
Analyzing
Applying

Materials
Food labels (see *Management 2*)
Calculators
Crayons or colored pencils
9" x 12" envelopes, seven
Small envelopes, one per student
Student pages

Background Information
The Nutrition Facts food label, jointly issued by the U.S. Department of Agriculture (USDA) and the Food and Drug Administration (FDA), is mandated for use on packaged foods and meat and poultry products. It features nutrients of current public health significance, uniform serving sizes, and recommended Daily Values.

This activity focuses on a major health concern—consumption of fat. The food label shows total calories and calories from fat per serving. It also lists the total grams of fat and grams of saturated fat. As of January 2006, the labels are also required to list the total grams of trans fat. Each fat gram equals nine calories. The Daily Values section gives the following recommendations concerning fats:

Calories	2000	2500
Total Fat	Less than 65 g	Less than 80 g
Saturated Fat	Less than 20 g	Less than 25 g

The Percent Daily Values listed by various nutrients are based on a 2000-calorie diet—the approximate calorie intake of elementary-aged children, depending on their activity level and other factors.

The USDA and FDA recommend that fat consumption be limited to a maximum of 35% of daily caloric intake; lower is better. Most fats should come from fish, nuts, and vegetable oils, which are either poly- or monounsaturated. Saturated fat should be no more than 10% of total calories. Trans fatty acids, which are even more harmful than saturated fats, should be avoided entirely, if possible. Because of the new FDA regulations requiring nutrition labels to list trans fat, its occurrence in foods will likely decrease as consumers become more aware of its presence and demand healthier alternatives.

Why be concerned about fat? Although fat does provide energy, diets high in fat heighten the risk of some types of cancer. Eating a high amount of trans fat or saturated fat (animal fat) can raise blood cholesterol, increasing the risk for heart disease. Unused fat calories are stored as fat, causing a problem with excess weight. Lowering the amount of fat consumed reduces these risks.

Management

1. For younger students, the first activity page is sufficient. For students ready to do more extensive work with percentages, continue with the second activity page, which reveals important information about individual foods.

2. Several weeks before doing the activity, ask students to bring in a variety of food labels from discarded packages at home. For an average-sized class, try to collect at least 150 labels, with representative samples from grains, vegetables, fruit, oils, milk, and meat and beans. Duplicates are needed because several students may choose certain foods, like milk. Don't forget butter, jam, mayonnaise, mustard, ketchup, and other condiments.

3. Write labels on seven 9" x 12" envelopes—one for the six food categories (see *Management 2)* and one for combination foods. Place these envelopes around the room and have students sort the food labels they bring in each day prior to the activity.

4. The day before the activity, set up the envelopes of food labels in an out-of-the-way place. While the regular curriculum continues, have one or two students at a time select from the labels to assemble a meal with three to eight foods. Provide them with small envelopes in which to store their choices. Do not tell them the purpose for choosing the food labels, other than it is for an activity they will be doing the next day.

Procedure

1. To set the stage, ask some preliminary questions:
   - Where do percentages appear in our daily lives? [basketball shooting, grades, chance of rain, school attendance goals, election results, public opinion polls, etc.]
   - What does a 50% chance of rain mean? [There is an even chance it will rain as it will not rain.]

   - If a basketball team shoots 37%, what does this mean? [For every hundred shots they take, 37 of the shots go in the basket.]
   - If every person in our class is here today, what is our attendance percentage? [100%]

2. Distribute the first activity page and instruct students to get the envelope of food labels they gathered yesterday. Then ask, "What percent of your meal do you think is fat?" Define the possible range by asking: "What is the lowest percentage possible?" [0%] and "What is the highest percentage possible?" [100%]. Have students write their estimates on the back of the activity page.

3. Have students read the food labels and record each food, the total calories, and the calories from fat.

4. Ask students to choose the appropriate method of calculation, then find and record the grand totals.

5. Have students follow the directions for coloring the two calorie bands.

6. Develop the concept of percent. Do not just give students the formula. Here is one possible way:

   "Look at your two calorie bands. How are the fat calories related to the total calories? Are they less than half (50%)? ...more than half? If they are less than 50%, that means your percent of fat is somewhere between 0 and ___? [49]. If they are over 50%, your percent will be between ___? [51 and 100]. Make a new estimate of the percent of calories from fat in your meal.

   "We have two categories—fat calories and total calories. Which one is the whole?" [total calories] Which one is part of the whole? [fat calories]

   "Here is a way we show the relationship between part and whole.

$$\frac{PART}{WHOLE}$$

   "When we substitute numbers for the words, we have a fraction. The middle line is a kind of dividing sign. For example:

$$\frac{PART}{WHOLE} = \frac{Fat\ calories}{Total\ calories} = \frac{70}{160}$$

   "We can divide the part (70) by the whole (160). The answer is 0.4375. Multiply that number by 100. Now we have 43.75. This is the percent of calories from fat. Let's round it to the nearest whole percent (44%)."

7. After the discussion, have students write the formula for finding percent in step 3 on their activity pages.

$$\frac{PART}{WHOLE} \times 100 = \%$$

   Then they should substitute their numbers and use a calculator to find the answer. Have them round to the nearest whole percent.

8. Distribute colored pencils and have students color in the percent band at the bottom of the page.
9. Finish with a class discussion or go on to the second page, if appropriate.
10. Give students the second activity page. Have them record each of their chosen foods, write the ratio of fat calories to total calories, calculate the percent, and color the fat bands.
11. Hold a concluding discussion.

Connecting Learning

1. What percentage of your meal came from fat?
2. The Food and Drug Administration recommends that no more than 35% of your daily calories come from fat. Given that the meal you chose would be one of three meals in a day, would you be able to meet this recommendation? Why or why not?
3. What substitutions could you make so that you would be able to meet this recommendation? (Try it and do the calculations.)
4. How does the amount of fat we eat affect our health? (See *Background Information*.)
5. Are some fats worse than others? [Yes. Saturated fats and trans fats are worse than polyunsaturated or monounsaturated fats.] Where are these bad fats found? [They are found in red meat and many processed, packaged foods like cookies and snacks.] Where are the "healthy" fats found? [fish, nuts, vegetable oils]
6. Why do some people ignore the amount of fat they eat? [They don't know where to find the information; they like a particular food too much to limit their eating of it; they see no immediate cause-and-effect link to poor health so why worry about it now.]

7. What foods were particularly high in fat? If we know about these foods and want to be healthy, what should we do about our eating habits? [We will eat these foods less often, although they do not need to be totally eliminated from our diet.]

Extensions

1. Make a circle percent graph of the same information. Compare it to the bar graph.
2. Find the percent of saturated and trans fat for each food. (Remember: There are nine calories per gram of fat, so number of grams of saturated fat x 9 calories = calories from saturated fats.) Discuss kinds of fat and health consequences.
3. Challenge the class to assemble desirable meals that are under the 35% limit. Repeat the activity with this goal in mind.
4. Compare percentages of fat among kinds of cheeses, milk, yogurt, ice cream, sour cream, or other similar foods.
5. Use chart paper to make lists of foods according to their percentages of fat. For younger students, label groups 0-29% and 30-100%. For older students, the categories could be 0-9%, 10-19%, 20-29%, etc. Add to the lists throughout the year.

Home Link

1. Encourage students to read food labels at home and to share their knowledge with their family. It could have an effect on the family diet.
2. Urge students to find out about health problems that may be related to diet.

* Reprinted with permission from *Principles and Standards for School Mathematics*, 2000 by the National Council of Teachers of Mathematics. All rights reserved.

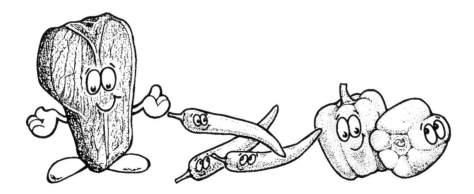

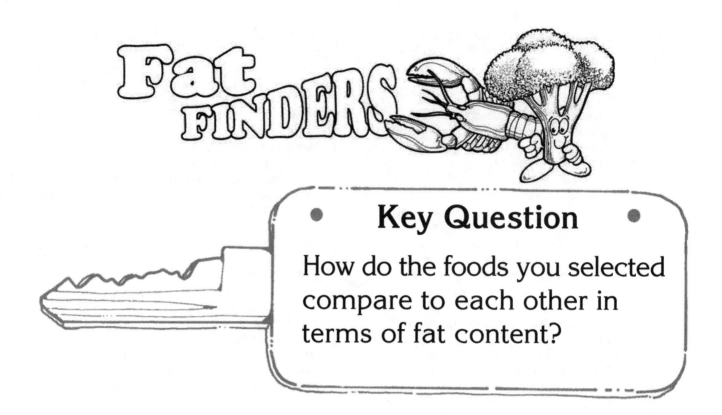

Fat FINDERS

Learning Goals

Students will:

- use food labels to determine the amount of fat in a meal they have chosen, and

- compare this to the recommended 35% limit of daily calories from fat.

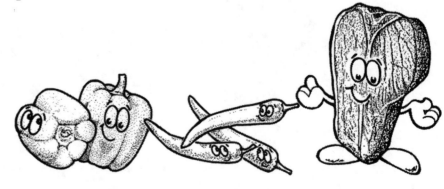

Fat FINDERS

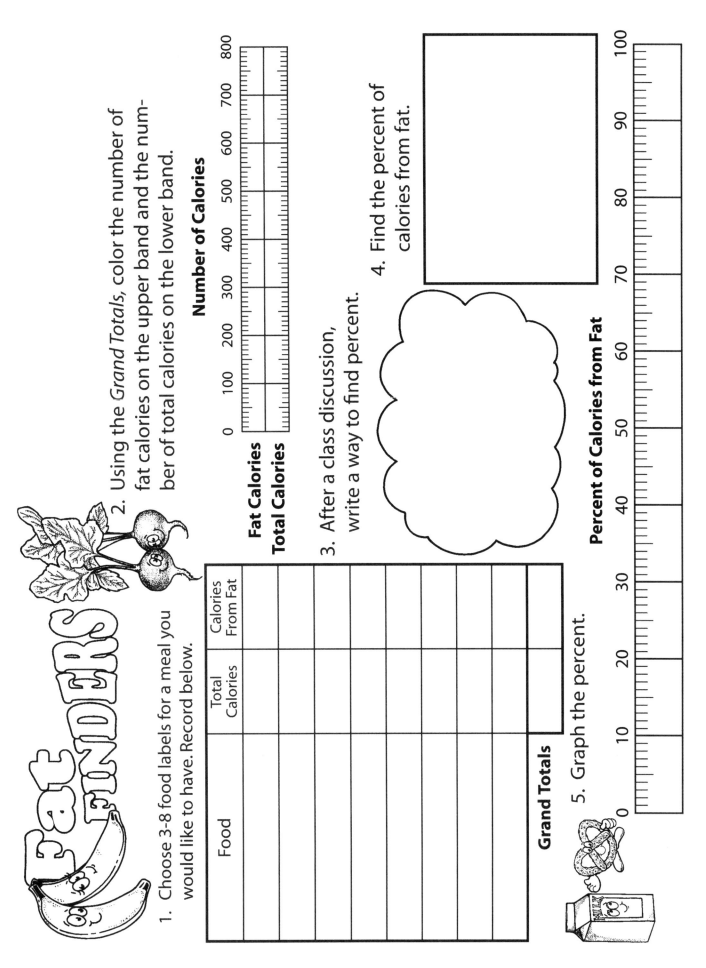

1. Choose 3-8 food labels for a meal you would like to have. Record below.

Food	Total Calories	Calories From Fat
Grand Totals		

2. Using the *Grand Totals*, color the number of fat calories on the upper band and the number of total calories on the lower band.

Number of Calories

Fat Calories	
Total Calories	

0 100 200 300 400 500 600 700 800

3. After a class discussion, write a way to find percent.

4. Find the percent of calories from fat.

5. Graph the percent.

Percent of Calories from Fat

0 10 20 30 40 50 60 70 80 90 100

Fat Finders

Fat Bars

Percent of Calories from Fat

Compare the amount of fat in each of the foods you chose.

Food	Total Calories	Calories From Fat

Connecting Learning

1. What percentage of your meal came from fat?

2. The Food and Drug Administration recommends that no more than 35% of your daily calories come from fat. Given that the meal you chose would be one of three meals in a day, would you be able to meet this recommendation? Why or why not?

3. What substitutions could you make so that you would be able to meet this recommendation?

4. How does the amount of fat we eat affect our health?

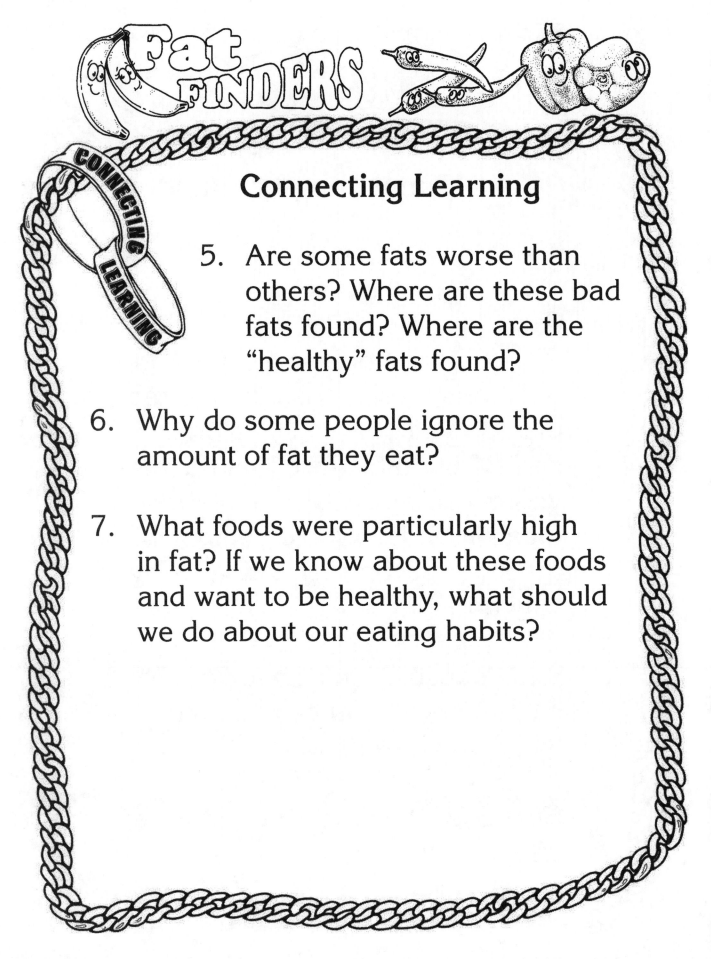

Connecting Learning

5. Are some fats worse than others? Where are these bad fats found? Where are the "healthy" fats found?

6. Why do some people ignore the amount of fat they eat?

7. What foods were particularly high in fat? If we know about these foods and want to be healthy, what should we do about our eating habits?

By Golly, By Gum

Topic
Food: sweeteners and flavorings in gum

Key Question
What happens to the mass of gum after it has been chewed for 10 minutes?

Learning Goals
Students will:
- use the scientific method to discover what happens to the mass of gum as it is chewed, and
- make a bar graph of data comparing the masses before and after chewing.

Guiding Documents
Project 2061 Benchmarks
- *No matter how parts of an object are assembled, the weight of the whole object made is always the same as the sum of the parts; and when a thing is broken into parts, the parts have the same total weight as the original thing.*
- *Measurements are always likely to give slightly different numbers, even if what is being measured stays the same.*

NRC Standards
- *Use appropriate tools and techniques to gather, analyze, and interpret data.*
- *Develop descriptions, explanations, predictions, and models using evidence.*
- *Think critically and logically to make the relationships between evidence and explanations.*

NCTM Standards 2000*
- *Understand such attributes as length, area, weight, volume, and size of angle and select the appropriate type of unit for measuring each attribute*
- *Collect data using observations, surveys, and experiments*
- *Represent data using tables and graphs such as line plots, bar graphs, and line graphs*

Math
Measurement
  mass

Whole number operations
Fractions
Percent
Graphs

Science
Life science
  health and nutrition
Physical science
  changes in matter

Integrated Processes
Observing
Predicting
Collecting and recording data
Interpreting data
Comparing and contrasting
Drawing conclusions
Generalizing

Materials
For each group:
  balance
  metric masses
  pack of gum (see *Management 5)*
  calculator
  crayons or markers

Background Information
There are three things that could happen to the mass of gum when it is chewed. One possibility is that the gum might gain mass since it is picking up saliva from the mouth. Another possibility is that the mass of the gum might stay the same since saliva is being added while sweeteners are being swallowed. A third possibility is that the mass of the gum will decrease since sweeteners and flavorings are being dissolved and swallowed.

What actually happens may be surprising. Sweeteners and flavorings provide the majority of the gum's mass. Most gums containing sugar lose 60-75% of their mass after being chewed for 10 minutes. Sugar-free gum will lose about 50% of its mass in 10 minutes. Gum labels list all ingredients by amount, with the substances having the greatest amount being listed first. The mass that is lost while gum is being chewed is dissolved in saliva and swallowed in the form of sugar and artificial flavorings. Many brands of gum contain more than one type of sugar, with corn syrup, dextrose, and glucose often listed as ingredients. Sugar-free gum will contain artificial sweeteners such as aspartame, sorbitol, or saccharin.

Management
1. *Caution: Be aware that the sugar in gum may cause problems for students with diabetes or hypoglycemia.*
2. Some teachers like to use the small, half-teaspoon sized sugar cubes instead of gram masses.
3. Students should work in groups of five so that each member chews one stick of gum.
4. Use a variety of brands and flavors of gum. Bubble gum works well since it has the greatest mass per piece to begin with and loses more mass than other types of gum.
5. While it is possible to find the before-and-after mass of individual pieces of gum, the results are much more accurate and impressive if the before-and-after mass of a pack of gum is found. For sanitary reasons, place the gum on the individual wrappers whenever finding the mass.
6. This activity has three parts, each taking 20-30 minutes. In *Part One*, students use the scientific method when they make and test their predictions. In *Part Two*, students use the data collected by each group to calculate the percent of sweetener and flavorings. In *Part Three*, students make a bar graph of the before-and-after masses of each group's pack of gum.
7. Overhead transparencies of the activity sheets are helpful for recording class data.

Procedure
Part One:
1. Discuss the *Key Question* and the three possible hypotheses (see *Background Information*).
2. Instruct students to record their predictions on the activity sheet.
3. Have the class discuss ways to test the predictions.
4. Decide on a class plan (or let each group come up with their own) for finding out what happens to the mass of gum after chewing. It is important that the before-and-after mass of the gum is quantified in some way so that *Part Two* of the activity can be done.
5. Have students record their plan. One such plan might direct each group to:
   a. Get a balance, masses, and a pack of gum.
   b. Save the outside wrapper for checking on ingredients later.
   c. Find and record the total mass of the five pieces of gum with individual wrappers.
   d. Chew the gum for 10 minutes and then put it back in the wrappers.
   e. Find and record the mass of the chewed gum.
   f. Analyze data to check predictions.

6. Have students do the activity.
7. Discuss the results. Students should share their predictions and how they were either validated or shown to need revision.
8. Direct students to read the list of ingredients on the outside labels of the various packs of gum and discuss what mass was lost in chewing.
9. Have students write their conclusions.

Part Two:
1. Hand out the activity page. Share and record the data for each group: brand, flavor, mass before chewing, and mass after chewing.
2. Have students do the calculations with or without a calculator for the difference, ratio, and percent of sweetener and flavorings in each pack of gum.
3. Discuss the results.

Part Three:
1. Have students construct a bar graph showing the mass before and after chewing for each pack of gum.
2. Discuss the graph.

Connecting Learning
Before doing the activity:
1. What *could* happen to the mass of gum as it is chewed? [increase, decrease, stay the same]
2. What *could* cause the mass to increase? ...decrease? ...stay the same?
3. How can you find out what happens?

After doing the activity:
1. What *does* happen to the mass of the gum after it is chewed for 10 minutes?
2. How can you explain this?
3. What are the ingredients in your pack of gum?
4. What ingredient in your gum has the most mass?
5. What do you think happens to this ingredient as you chew? How can you tell?
6. How did the brand or flavor of gum affect the amount of mass lost?
7. What does your graph tell you?
8. What other questions can you think of that stem from this activity?

Extensions
1. Do *By Golly, By Gum, By Time.*
2. Chew gum for 20 minutes; compare results.
3. Do the activity using different types of gum, including sugar-free.
4. Students can make math word problems from data.

* Reprinted with permission from *Principles and Standards for School Mathematics,* 2000 by the National Council of Teachers of Mathematics. All rights reserved.

By Golly, By Gum

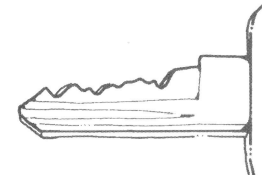

Key Question

What happens to the mass of gum after it has been chewed for 10 minutes?

Learning Goals

Students will:

- investigate what happens to the mass of gum as it is chewed, and

- make a bar graph of data comparing the masses before and after chewing.

By Golly, By Gum

Part One

What happens to the mass of gum after it is chewed for 10 minutes?

Prediction: I think the mass will _____ because

Plan for testing your prediction on the back of this paper.

Results:

    Mass of gum before chewing _____

    Mass of gum after chewing _____

Conclusions:

By Golly, By Gum
Part Two

How much sweetener & flavorings are in gum?

Brand	Flavor	Total Mass of Pack (grams)	Chewed Mass of Pack (grams)	Difference	Ratio $\frac{Difference}{Total}$	% Sweetener & Flavorings Ratio x 100 = %
1.						
2.						
3.						
4.						
5.						
6.						
7.						

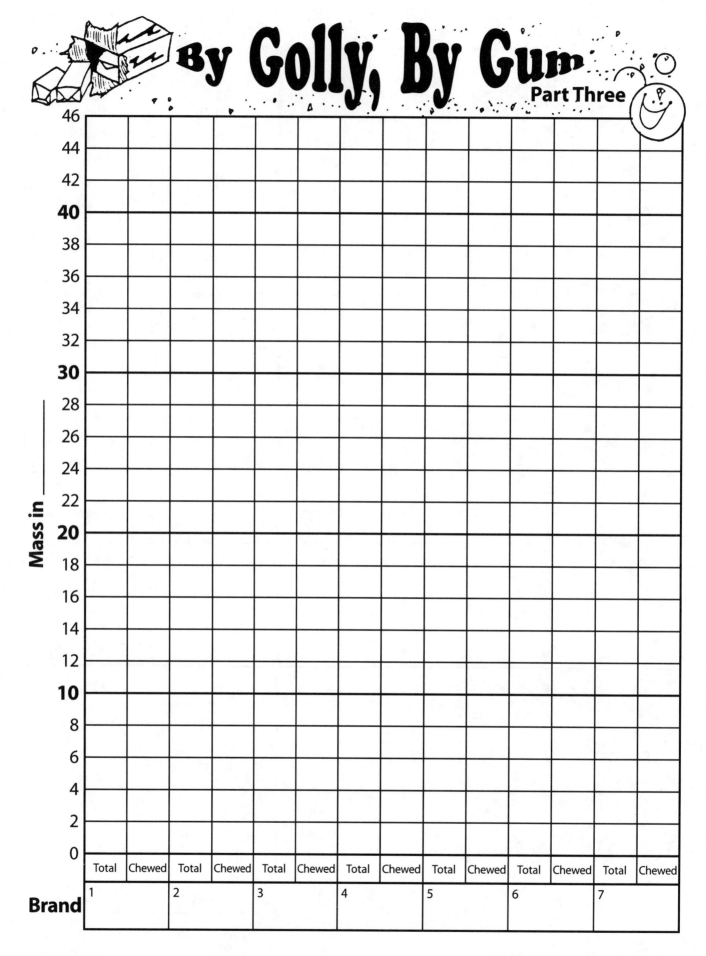

By Golly, By Gum

Part Three

Mass in _____

46
44
40
38
36
34
32
30
28
26
24
22
20
18
16
14
12
10
8
6
4
2
0

Total	Chewed	Total	Chewed	Total	Chewed	Total	Chewed	Total	Chewed	Total	Chewed	Total	Chewed
1		2		3		4		5		6		7	

Brand

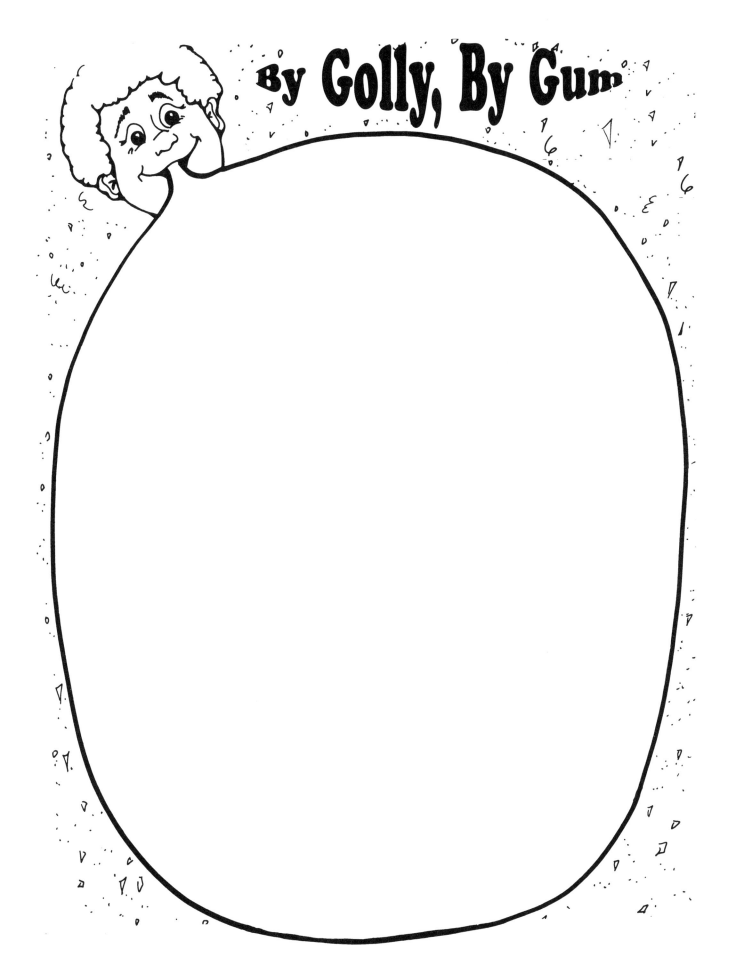

By Golly, By Gum

By Golly, By Gum

Connecting Learning

1. What could happen to the mass of gum as it is chewed?

2. What does happen to the mass of the gum after it is chewed for 10 minutes?

3. What are the ingredients in your pack of gum?

4. What ingredient in your gum has the most mass?

5. What do you think happens to this ingredient as you chew? How can you tell?

By Golly, By Gum

Connecting Learning

6. How did the brand or flavor of gum affect the amount of mass lost?

7. What does your graph tell you?

8. What other questions can you think of that stem from this activity?

By Golly, By Gum, By Time

Topic
Food: changes in matter

Key Question
How does the amount of time gum is chewed affect its mass?

Learning Goals
Students will:
- chew gum to see what happens to its mass, and
- discover how the mass of the gum is affected by the amount of time it is chewed.

Guiding Documents
Project 2061 Benchmarks
- *Measuring instruments can be used to gather accurate information for making scientific comparisons of objects and events and for designing and constructing things that will work properly.*
- *Things change in steady, repetitive, or irregular ways—or sometimes in more than one way at the same time. Often the best way to tell which kinds of change are happening is to make a table or graph of measurements.*

NRC Standard
- *Objects have many observable properties, including size, weight, shape, color, temperature, and the ability to react with other substances. Those properties can be measured using tools, such as rulers, balances, and thermometers.*

NCTM Standards 2000*
- *Understand such attributes as length, area, weight, volume, and size of angle and select the appropriate type of unit for measuring each attribute*
- *Collect data using observations, surveys, and experiments*
- *Represent data using tables and graphs such as line plots, bar graphs, and line graphs*

Math
Measurement
    mass
Graphs

Science
Physical science
    changes in matter
Life science
    health and nutrition

Integrated Processes
Observing
Predicting
Collecting and organizing data
Comparing and contrasting
Drawing conclusions

Materials
For each group:
    balance
    metric masses
    pack of gum
    rulers, one per student

For the class:
    timer or clock with second hand

Background Information
Gum labels list all ingredients by mass, with the substances having the most mass being listed first. Sweetener and flavorings provide the majority of gum's mass. The mass that is lost in chewing is swallowed in the form of sweetener and flavorings.

In doing this activity, it is interesting to discover that most of the loss of mass occurs in the first few minutes of chewing. In fact, some gums lose more than half their mass in the first two minutes! Gum will continue to lose mass as it is being chewed until all the sweetener and flavorings are dissolved and swallowed.

After being chewed for 10 minutes, most gums containing sugar lose 60-75% of their mass, while sugar-free gums lose about 50%. The mass will stabilize and remain constant after 10-20 minutes of chewing since only the gum base is left. This loss of mass can be displayed effectively on a broken-line graph, a type of graph that is often used to show changes over time.

Management
1. This activity is designed as a follow-up for *By Golly, By Gum.*
2. Students should work in groups of five so that each student chews one stick of gum.

112

3 Use a variety of different types (including sugar-free), brands, and flavors of gum. This will allow students to compare results from the data collected.

4. Have students save both the outside wrapper of their pack of gum and the individual wrappers from each piece of gum. The outside wrappers will later be used to check the list of ingredients and the individual wrappers will be used each time they find the mass of the gum.

5. Since students will chew and find the mass of the gum several times, they either need to write their names on their wrappers or place their gum in the same spot on the balance pan each time (see illustration). Minimize sticking problems by placing the gum on open wrappers rather than closing the wrappers around the gum.

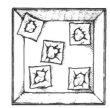

6. In constructing the broken-line graph, students need to pick an appropriate scale for the vertical axis. This scale will vary according to the total mass of each pack of gum.

Procedure

Part One

1. Discuss the *Key Question*: "How does the amount of time gum is chewed affect its mass?"
2. Distribute gum, balances, masses, and the *Part One* activity sheet to each group.
3. Instruct each group to carefully remove the gum pack's outer wrapper and put it aside for later use.
4. Have each group find the total mass of the five pieces of gum with individual wrappers. Record this mass under *zero* in the table.
5. Tell students to chew the gum for two minutes, put the gum back in the individual wrappers, find the total mass of the five pieces again, and record under the *two* in the table.
6. Have students repeat the above process four more times and record the data.
7. Discuss the findings.
8. Have groups read the ingredients in their gums and discuss how these ingredients affect the mass that was lost.
9. Provide time for students to write their conclusions in the space provided.

Part Two

1. Distribute rulers and the *Part Two* activity sheet to each group.
2. Have each group pick an appropriate scale for the vertical axis (mass of gum) that will allow their data to be graphed. Stress the need to use as much of the graph paper as possible.
3. Have students graph their group's data and then have each group share results.
4. Discuss the graphs.
5. Have students answer the question about their graph found at the bottom of the first student page.

Connecting Learning

Part One

1. What happens to the mass of gum after it is chewed?
2. How does the variable of time chewed affect the mass of gum?
3. What is happening to the mass that is lost?
4. What are the ingredients in your pack of gum?
5. What ingredient in your gum has the most mass?
6. What do the ingredients tell you about the mass lost?

Part Two

1. Does gum lose mass at a steady rate when it is chewed? Explain.
2. Will the mass of the gum ever remain constant while being chewed? Why or why not?
3. Did the type or brand of gum affect the amount of mass lost? Explain.
4. How did the taste of the gum change as it was being chewed? Is there a correlation between taste and mass?
5. What other questions can you think of that stem from this activity?

Extensions

1. Do the activity using one-minute intervals and compare results.
2. Do the activity for longer than 10 minutes and graph the results.
3. Graph the results for several groups on one graph.

*   Reprinted with permission from *Principles and Standards for School Mathematics*, 2000 by the National Council of Teachers of Mathematics. All rights reserved.

By Golly, By Gum, By Time

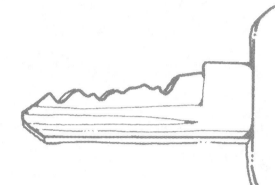

Key Question

How does the amount of time gum is chewed affect its mass?

Learning Goals

Students will:

- chew gum to see what happens to its mass, and

- discover how the mass of the gum is affected by the amount of time it is chewed.

By Golly, By Gum, By Time

Part One

How does the amount of time gum is chewed affect its mass?

I think the mass will _____ because

Record the total mass of your pack of gum, including individual wrappers, at the beginning (0) and then after every two minutes of chewing.

Time chewed in minutes	0	2	4	6	8	10
Mass in grams						

Conclusions:

Use the following page to graph your results as a broken line graph. What does your graph tell you about how the mass of the gum changed as it was chewed?

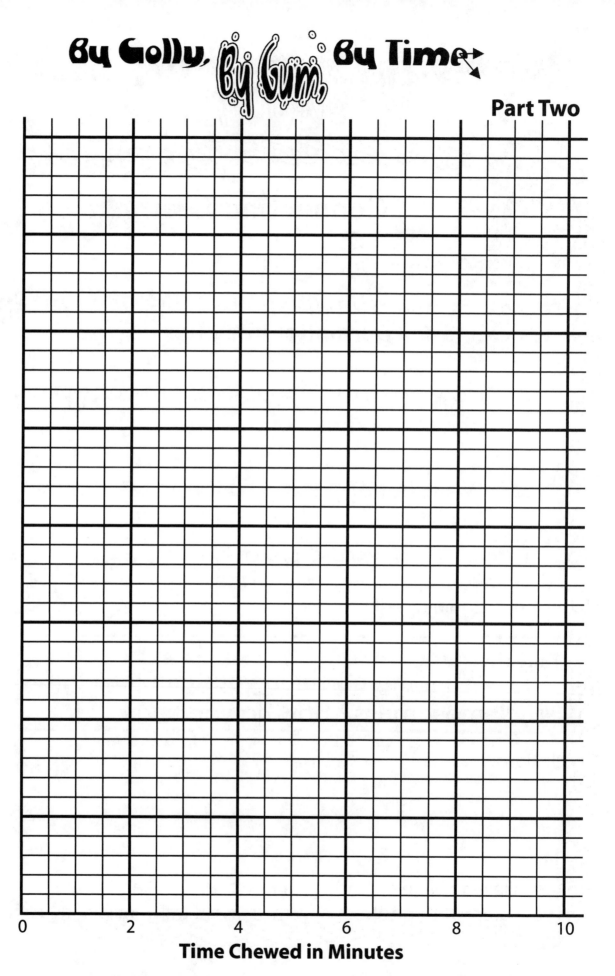

By Golly, By Gum, By Time

Part Two

Mass of Gum in Grams

Time Chewed in Minutes

0   2   4   6   8   10

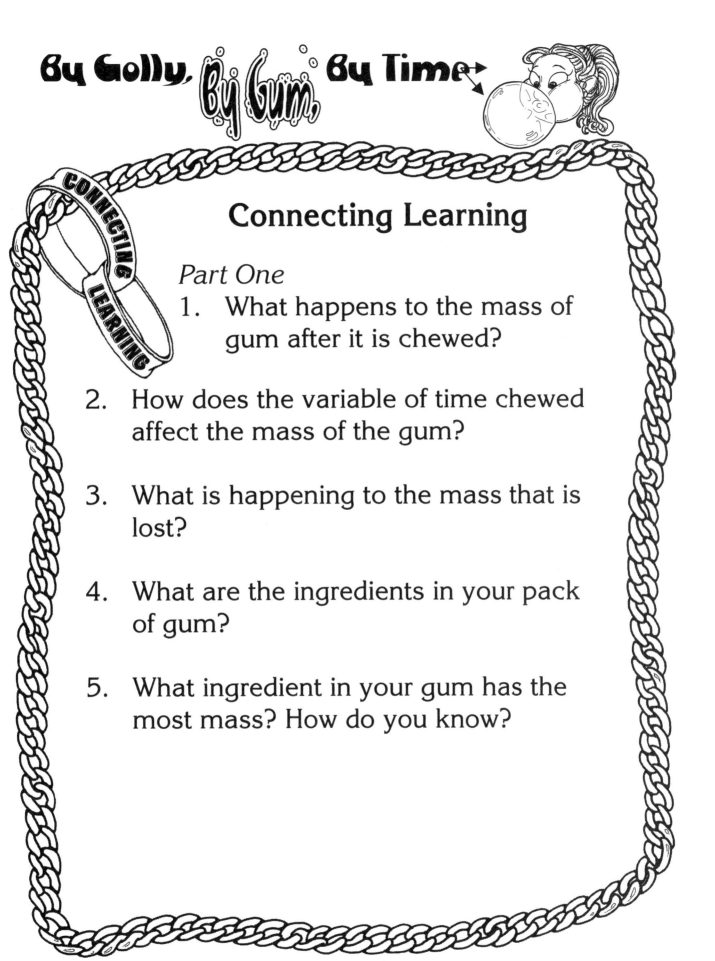

Connecting Learning

Part One

1. What happens to the mass of gum after it is chewed?

2. How does the variable of time chewed affect the mass of the gum?

3. What is happening to the mass that is lost?

4. What are the ingredients in your pack of gum?

5. What ingredient in your gum has the most mass? How do you know?

Connecting Learning

Part Two

1. Does gum lose mass at a steady rate when it is chewed? Explain.

2. Will the mass of the gum ever remain constant while being chewed? Why do you think this?

3. Did the type or brand of gum affect the amount of mass lost? Explain.

4. How did the taste of the gum change as it was being chewed? Is there a relationship between the taste of the gum and its mass? Explain.

5. What other questions can you think of that stem from this activity?

Candy Factory

Topic
Food packaging/proportionality

Key Questions
1. How do different packages of the same kind of candy compare?
2. How can we divide the candy so everyone has the same amount of each color?

Learning Goals
Students will:
• compare the color distribution within packages of candy, and
• divide them into fair shares.

Guiding Documents
Project 2061 Benchmarks
• *Finding out what the biggest and the smallest possible values of something are is often as revealing as knowing what the usual value is.*
• *Use numerical data in describing and comparing objects and events.*

NCTM Standards 2000*
• *Understand the effects of multiplying and dividing whole numbers*
• *Develop understanding of fractions as parts of unit wholes, as parts of a collection, as locations on number lines, and as divisions of whole numbers*
• *Collect data using observations, surveys, and experiments*
• *Represent data using tables and graphs such as line plots, bar graphs, and line graphs*

Math
Estimation
Counting
Whole number operations
Fractions
Ranges
Graphs

Integrated Processes
Observing
Classifying
Collecting and recording data
Comparing and contrasting
Generalizing

Materials
For each group:
　1 small bag of candy (see *Management 1*)
　dinner knife
　crayons

Background Information
　Manufacturers strive for a fairly consistent distribution of colored candies within a particular package. Though variations do occur, they are slight enough to allow generalizations about the total number and the relative frequency of the various colors.

　Proportionality is one of the major concepts in mathematics. In the second part of this activity, students will divide candies to form proportions, strengthening their concept of the division process.

　Division is the process of completing a proportion. In this activity, the number one is used in the upper left to give meaning to the quotient and complete a proportion. For example, the following illustrations show how 14 candies will look after being divided into four fair shares on the *Fair Shares* mat and the corresponding record that can be written.

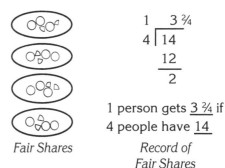

Fair Shares　　　*Record of Fair Shares*

1 person gets 3 ¾ if
4 people have 14

　Each group member gets the candies in one of the ovals and the leftovers are cut into fourths and evenly distributed. In this example, each person would each receive three and two-fourths candies.

Management

1. All groups should use the same package size and type of candy, one that comes in a variety of colors.
2. This activity is designed for groups of four.

Procedure

Count by Color:

1. Ask the first *Key Question* and record student responses.
2. Divide the class into groups of four and give them the *Count by Color* page. Each group should be identified by a letter, starting with letter A.
3. Show the class one bag of candy and have students estimate and record the number of candies in the bag.
4. Distribute one bag to each group. After opening the bags, have the class record the colors in the same order in the table.
5. Instruct groups to count by color and record in their group column.
6. Have students calculate the total number of candies, recheck by actually counting the candies, and record the actual number next to their estimate.
7. As the groups report their results, instruct students to record the count for each color in the table, then illustrate the data on the *Class Graph*.
8. Give students the *Class Results* page and have them label it with the color names.
9. After locating the lowest and highest count for each color from the table or *Class Graph*, have students color that range on the number line. For example, if the lowest count for orange is four and the highest is nine, students would color the band between four and nine.
10. Discuss the results.

Fair Shares:

1. Ask the second *Key Question*. Give students the *Fair Shares* and *Record of Fair Shares* pages.
2. Havea each group place all the candies of one color in the candy factory on the *Fair Shares* sheet. Have them divide the candies among the four ovals and make a record on the *Record of Fair Shares* sheet. When there are no longer enough whole candies to divide evenly, have students use a dinner knife to cut the remaining candies into fourths. These pieces should be distributed among the ovals and recorded as fractions (see *Background Information*).
3. Tell each group member to take the candies in one of the ovals.
4. Follow the same procedure for each color and discuss the results.
5. Let students eat the candies.

Connecting Learning

1. How are the packages of candy the same? [same colors, same wrappers, etc.]
2. How are the packages of candy different? [different numbers of each color, different total amount, etc.]
3. How do the amounts of each color compare?
4. Is there one color that dominates the mix? If so, which one?
5. Which color has the largest range? ...the smallest range?
6. Look at the range for each color of candy. What number would be in the middle or about the middle of that range?
7. After dividing into fair shares, how many total candies did you receive?
8. What did you notice about the leftovers? (Some may have observed that ¾ is the same as ½.)
9. Write several true statements based on your results.

Extensions

1. Find the average number of candies in a bag and/or the average number of each color. Rank the colors according to frequency.
2. Find the mass of the orange candies, yellow candies, etc. Compare the mass to the number counted.

Curriculum Correlation

Art

Have students draw a series of sequential pictures showing their own concept of how the candies are made and the packages filled in a factory assembly line. A cartoon format could be used.

Candy Factory

Key Questions

1. How do packages of the same kind of candy compare?
2. How can we divide the candy so everyone has the same amount of each color?

Learning Goals

Students will:

- compare the color distribution within packages of candy, and

- divide them into fair shares.

Candy Factory
Count and Color

Total number of candies in your bag:

Estimate _____ Actual _____

Class Results

Color	A	B	C	D	E	F	G	H	I

Groups

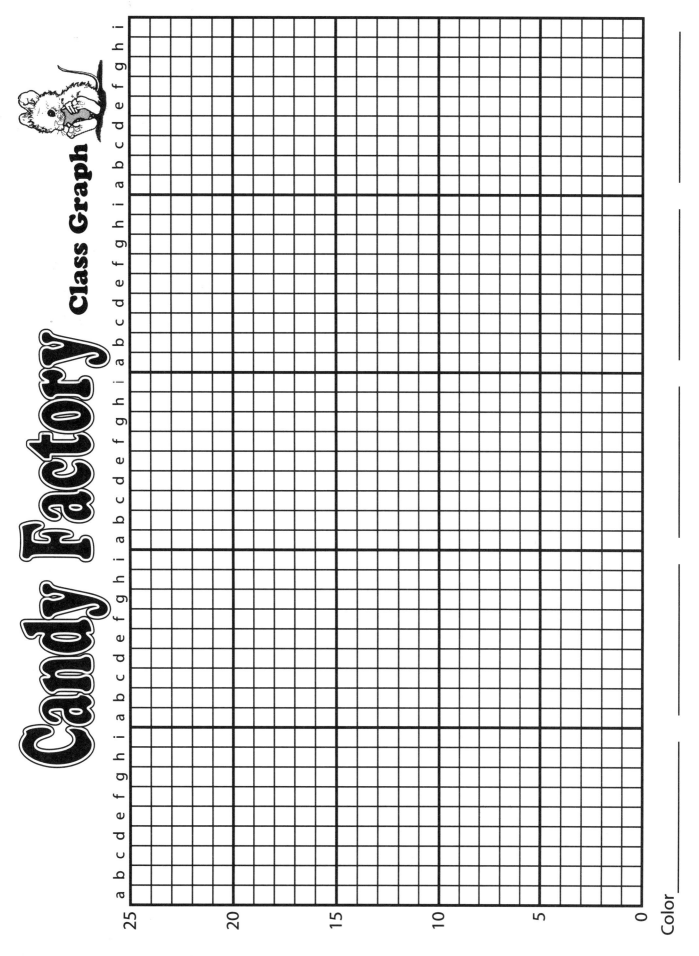

Candy Factory Class Graph

25

20

15

10

5

0

Color _____

123

Candy Factory

Class Results
Range of Count

Color: ___

0 1 2 3 4 5 6 7 8 9 10 11 12 13 14 15 16 17 18 19 20

Color: ___

0 1 2 3 4 5 6 7 8 9 10 11 12 13 14 15 16 17 18 19 20

Color: ___

0 1 2 3 4 5 6 7 8 9 10 11 12 13 14 15 16 17 18 19 20

Color: ___

0 1 2 3 4 5 6 7 8 9 10 11 12 13 14 15 16 17 18 19 20

Color: ___

0 1 2 3 4 5 6 7 8 9 10 11 12 13 14 15 16 17 18 19 20

Color: ___

0 1 2 3 4 5 6 7 8 9 10 11 12 13 14 15 16 17 18 19 20

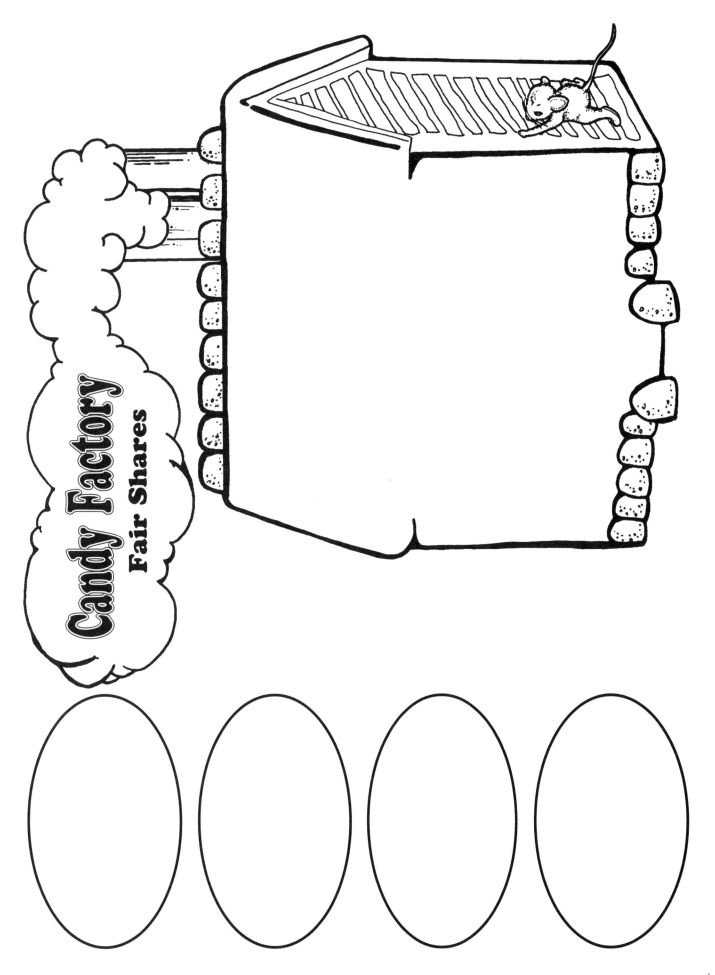

Candy Factory
Fair Shares

Candy Factory
Record of Fair Shares

1
4⌐

1 person gets _____ if
4 people have _____.

_____
color

1
4⌐

1 person gets _____ if
4 people have _____.

_____
color

1
4⌐

1 person gets _____ if
4 people have _____.

_____
color

1
4⌐

1 person gets _____ if
4 people have _____.

_____
color

1
4⌐

1 person gets _____ if
4 people have _____.

_____
color

1
4⌐

1 person gets _____ if
4 people have _____.

_____
color

JAW BREAKERS AND HEART THUMPERS   126   © 2006 AIMS EDUCATION FOUNDATION

Candy Factory

Connecting Learning

1. How are the packages of candy the same?

2. How are the packages of candy different?

3. How do the amounts of each color compare?

4. Is there one color that dominates the mix? If so, which one?

5. Which color has the largest range? ...the smallest range?

Candy Factory

Connecting Learning

6. Look at the range for each color of candy. What number would be in the middle or about the middle of that range?

7. After dividing into fair shares, how many total candies did you receive?

8. What did you notice about the leftovers?

9. Write several true statements based on your results.

Water IN APPLES

Topic
Food dehydration: apples

Key Question
How will the mass of the apples change after four days?

Learning Goals
Students will:
- graph changes in apples using either a bar graph or line graph,
- follow a set of written instructions for a scientific investigation, and
- use data and graphs from the investigation to explain what happened to the water in the apples.

Guiding Documents
Project 2061 Benchmarks
- *Things change in steady, repetitive, or irregular ways—or sometimes in more than one way at the same time. Often the best way to tell which kinds of change are happening is to make a table or graph of measurements.*
- *Use numerical data in describing and comparing objects and events.*
- *Results of similar scientific investigations seldom turn out exactly the same. Sometimes this is because of unexpected differences in the things being investigated, sometimes because of unrealized differences in the methods used or in the circumstances in which the investigation is carried out, and sometimes just because of uncertainties in observations. It is not always easy to tell which.*
- *Keep records of their investigations and observations and not change the records later.*

NRC Standard
- *Objects have many observable properties, including size, weight, shape, color, temperature, and the ability to react with other substances. Those properties can be measured using tools, such as rulers, balances, and thermometers.*

NCTM Standards 2000*
- *Select and apply appropriate standard units and tools to measure length, area, volume, weight, time, temperature, and the size of angles*
- *Collect data using observations, surveys, and experiments*
- *Represent data using tables and graphs such as line plots, bar graphs, and line graphs*

Math
Measurement
    mass
Whole number operations
Averages
Data analysis
    graphing

Science
Physical science
    changes in matter

Integrated Processes
Observing
Predicting
Collecting and recording data
Comparing and contrasting
Controlling variables
Generalizing

Materials
For each group:
    3 apples of uniform size (whole, peeled, chopped)
    balance
    gram masses
    3 pieces of waxed paper or paper towel
    peeler
    plastic serrated knife

Background Information
Apples are about 84% water. The speed with which this moisture evaporates into the air depends on the amount of exposed surface and the relative humidity. In very humid environments, it is possible for the apples to gain moisture. The chopped apple should

lose the most moisture. The peeled apple should show a significant loss. The whole, unpeeled apple should show minimal loss because of the protection offered by the skin.

People who eat apples are receiving vitamin A and some vitamin C. They are also helping to replenish the body's water supply.

Management
1. Divide the class into groups of three to five students.
2. Student groups or the teacher should prepare the apples in class. It is helpful to set the apples on individual pieces of waxed paper or paper towel.
3. The first measurement of mass must occur *after* preparation. The pieces of waxed paper or paper towel on which the apples are placed should be included each time the mass is found.
4. Apples may be placed by a window or outdoors (be aware of insects). Apples dried outdoors should be brought in at the end of the day.
5. Allow five consecutive days for the activity.
   a. *Monday* (45-60 minutes): introduction and preparation of apples
   b. *Tues., Wed., Thurs.* (15-20 minutes): measuring
   c. *Friday* (45-60 minutes): measuring, graphing, drawing conclusions
6. Measuring and recording should occur every day at the same time.

Procedure
Monday-Thursday
1. Have each group prepare the three apples. Then, on the first activity sheet, have each student record his or her observations about one of the apples.
2. Ask the *Key Question* and, on the second activity sheet, have students record their predictions for which apple will lose the most moisture.
3. Instruct students to find the mass of each apple—the unpeeled, the peeled, and the chopped—every day. Record the results and figure the loss.

Friday
1. Have students graph the masses using either the line graph or the bar graph. Line graphs are used to show change over time.
2. Ask students to find the total loss of each kind of apple by adding the differences or subtracting Friday's mass from Monday's mass.
3. On the first activity sheet, have students write observations about the condition of the same apple that was observed on Monday.
4. Discuss the differences in loss of moisture and, on the first activity sheet, have students write conclusions based on the graph.

Connecting Learning
1. What did you discover while doing this activity?
2. When did your group's apples lose the most mass? How do you know?
3. Why was it important to find the mass of the apples at the same time each day?
4. What kind of information did your graph give you about the changes you observed?
5. Why is it important for you to follow directions when conducting a scientific investigation?
6. What are you wondering now?

Extensions
1. Extend the activity over a longer period of time until no further loss of moisture occurs. Discuss what to do about weekend measurements. Make a line graph on graph paper.
2. Try this activity during another season and compare results.
3. Use this procedure with a different fruit and compare results.
4. Complete the *In Search of Apples* page.

* Reprinted with permission from *Principles and Standards for School Mathematics*, 2000 by the National Council of Teachers of Mathematics. All rights reserved.

Water IN APPLES

Key Question

How will the mass of apples change after four days?

Learning Goals

Students will:

- graph changes in apples using either a bar graph or line graph,

- follow a set of written instructions for a scientific investigation, and

- use data and graphs from the investigation to explain what happened to the water in the apples.

Water IN Apples

OBSERVING

Pick one of the apples (unpeeled, peeled, or chopped) and describe how it *looks, feels,* and *smells.*

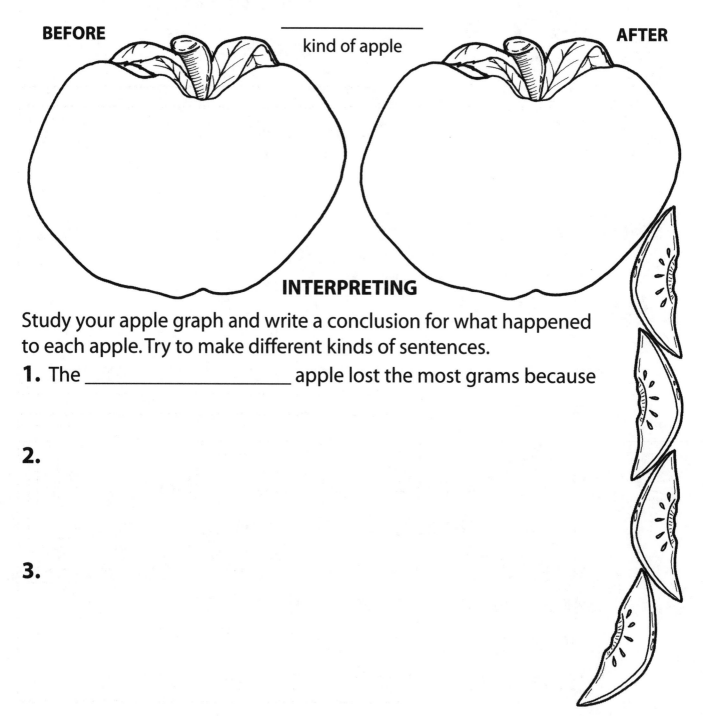

BEFORE

_____
kind of apple

AFTER

INTERPRETING

Study your apple graph and write a conclusion for what happened to each apple. Try to make different kinds of sentences.

1. The _____ apple lost the most grams because

2.

3.

Water in Apples

I predict the _____ apple will lose the most water.

Unpeeled

Difference

Mon. _____ g g

Tues. _____ g g

Wed. _____ g g

Thurs. _____ g g

Fri. _____ g g

Total Loss _____ g

Peeled

Difference

Mon. _____ g g

Tues. _____ g g

Wed. _____ g g

Thurs. _____ g g

Fri. _____ g g

Total Loss _____ g

Chopped

Difference

Mon. _____ g g

Tues. _____ g g

Wed. _____ g g

Thurs. _____ g g

Fri. _____ g g

Total Loss _____ g

Water IN Apples

Bar Graphs

Unpeeled

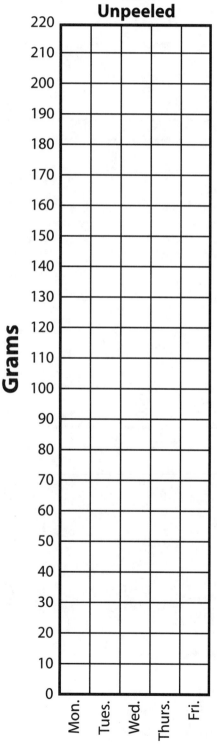

Grams

220
210
200
190
180
170
160
150
140
130
120
110
100
90
80
70
60
50
40
30
20
10
0

Mon. Tues. Wed. Thurs. Fri.

Peeled

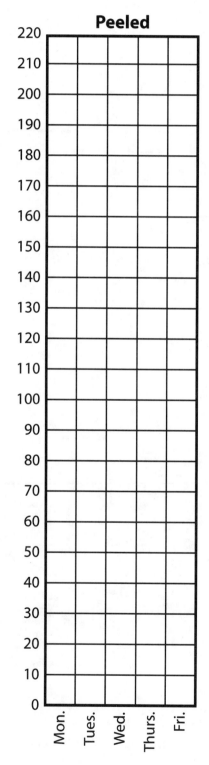

220
210
200
190
180
170
160
150
140
130
120
110
100
90
80
70
60
50
40
30
20
10
0

Mon. Tues. Wed. Thurs. Fri.

Chopped

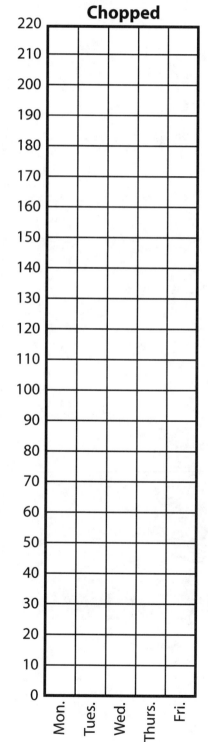

220
210
200
190
180
170
160
150
140
130
120
110
100
90
80
70
60
50
40
30
20
10
0

Mon. Tues. Wed. Thurs. Fri.

Water IN APPLES

LINE GRAPH

Record each apple's mass by making a point on the thick line for every day. Connect the points, in order from Monday to Friday, with straight lines. Use a different color for each kind of apple.

In Search of Apples

1. Go to the fresh produce section of your grocery store. Write down all the different kinds of apples you find and complete the table.

Kind of Apple	Price per lb.	Color	Size (S-M-L)

2. How many kinds of products made from apples can you find in the store? How are they packaged?

	PACKAGE			
	Box/ Carton	Can/Jar	Bag	Other
applesauce		✓		

Water IN Apples

Connecting Learning

1. What did you discover while doing this activity?

2. When did your group's apples lose the most mass? How do you know?

3. Why was it important to find the mass of the apples at the same time each day?

4. What kind of information did your graph give you about the changes you observed?

5. Why is it important for you to follow directions when conducting a scientific investigation?

6. What are you wondering now?

Cut and Dried

Topic
Food dehydration

Key Question
Which food will lose the most mass?

Learning Goal
Students will learn about the comparative amounts of water in foods.

Guiding Documents
Project 2061 Benchmarks
- *Things change in steady, repetitive, or irregular ways—or sometimes in more than one way at the same time. Often the best way to tell which kinds of change are happening is to make a table or graph of measurements.*
- *Measurements are always likely to give slightly different numbers, even if what is being measured stays the same.*
- *Use numerical data in describing and comparing objects and events.*
- *Keep records of their investigations and observations and not change the records later.*

NRC Standard
- *Objects have many observable properties, including size, weight, shape, color, temperature, and the ability to react with other substances. Those properties can be measured using tools, such as rulers, balances, and thermometers.*

NCTM Standards 2000*
- *Select and apply appropriate standard units and tools to measure length, area, volume, weight, time, temperature, and the size of angles*
- *Collect data using observations, surveys, and experiments*
- *Represent data using tables and graphs such as line plots, bar graphs, and line graphs*

Math
Measurement
    mass
Order
Whole number operations

Science
Life science
    health and nutrition
Physical science
    changes in matter

Integrated Processes
Observing
Predicting
Collecting and recording data
Controlling variables
Comparing and contrasting

Materials
For each group:
    balance
    gram masses
    serrated, plastic knife

For the class:
    waxed paper
    5 different fruits and vegetables (see *Management 1*)
    sharp knife
    potato peeler
    cutting board

Background Information
Foods contain varying amounts of water, usually a surprising percent of their total mass. Fruits generally contain more water than vegetables. The water in foods is one way we replace water lost through sweating, urination, etc. Our body, being about 60% water, needs water to maintain its functions.

The amount of exposed surface on food determines the rate of dehydration. To control this variable, all foods should be peeled and have roughly the same shape and size.

By starting with the same beginning mass, comparisons between foods can be made without dealing with percents. However, measurements can never be exact. In reality, the pieces of food will be cut close, but not exactly to the beginning targeted mass. Mass will also probably be estimated to the nearest gram or half gram. Careful and accurate readings when finding the mass help minimize these factors.

If you do this activity in an extremely humid environment, it is possible for the food pieces to gain mass. If you think this might be a possibility, you may want to control humidity in some way or plan to do it at a time of year when humidity is relatively low.

Management
1. Each group will need five foods. All groups will use the same five foods. Choose a combination of fruits and vegetables such as potatoes, peppers, squash, eggplant, apples, bananas, persimmons, pears, melons, etc.
2. Ask students to bring two of each kind of food; this allows for mistakes such as cutting below the mass wanted.
3. Decide the target mass (all food pieces will be cut to this mass) before doing the activity. Ten to 20 grams is recommended.
4. Peel and cut chunks of each food for every group. Make sure the pieces have more mass than the targeted mass.
5. Groups of five work well since each person will be responsible for one of the five foods.
6. This activity is divided into two parts. Predicting, cutting foods, and finding their mass will take about 60 minutes. After a two-day waiting period, finding the dehydrated mass and ordering the results will take about 45 minutes.

Procedure
Part One
1. Give students the first activity page. Have them predict and record which food will lose the most mass, ordering the other foods beneath it.
2. Tell students the target mass. Have them record the mass and mutliply this by the number of groups to determine the class total mass for each food.
3. Demonstrate how to cut a food piece, find its mass, cut more, find its mass, etc., until the targeted mass is obtained.
4. Discuss how variables are being controlled (see *Connecting Learning*).
5. Distribute the food chunks, plastic knives, balances, and gram masses to each group. Have them trim the prepared chunks to the targeted mass. Each student within the group can be responsible for a different food. Masses may need to be double-checked.
6. Give each group a letter from A to F. Have groups place their food slices in separate areas on pieces of waxed paper labeled with the group's letter. Set the food aside and wait two days.

Part Two
1. Have student groups gather a balance, gram masses, and their food pieces. They should find the mass of each food and record it in their group's column in the table on the first page.
2. Share results so students can record data from all the groups and add the totals for each food.
3. Give students the second activity page and have them construct a graph showing the class total for

beginning mass (the same for each food) and the class totals for the ending mass of each food. The number increments should be written in the space between the two graphs. The same increments must be used for both graphs to make comparisons.
4. Have students find the difference between the class totals for beginning and ending mass of each food. They should write their computations along with the appropriate food label in the space provided.
5. Instruct students to write the foods in order of actual mass lost next to their predictions on the first activity page.
6. Discuss the results.

Connecting Learning
1. What are we doing to keep testing conditions the same? [Controlling the amount of exposed surface by peeling foods and cutting them roughly the same size and shape. Taking accurate measurements when finding mass and starting with a beginning mass as close as possible to the targeted mass.]
2. How could the results change if these controls are not used? [The amount of exposed surface will change the rate of dehydration. Inaccurate measurements or varying beginning masses can change how the foods compare.]
3. What do foods lose when they are dried? [water]
4. Which contain more water, fruits or vegetables? [usually fruits]
5. What food(s) do you think might beat the mass loss winner? (Go ahead. Run another test.)
6. Do you think our foods still have water in them? (Let students extend the time of the activity to explore this. Dried foods still contain some water; dehydrated foods contain a very small amount also.)
7. Why is the water in foods important to people? [Our body is about 60% water. Eating foods is one way to replenish the water we lose through sweating, elimination of wastes, etc.]

Extensions
1. Find the average loss of each food.
2. Buy some dehydrated food such as backpackers use. Fix it and taste.

Curriculum Correlation
Language Arts
   Have students search for synonyms for *drying* such as evaporate, dehydrate, sweat, etc.

Social Science
1. Research how people, past and present, preserve foods by drying.
2. Find out about food the astronauts eat while in space.

* Reprinted with permission from *Principles and Standards for School Mathematics*, 2000 by the National Council of Teachers of Mathematics. All rights reserved.

Cut and Dried

Key Question

Which food will lose the most mass?

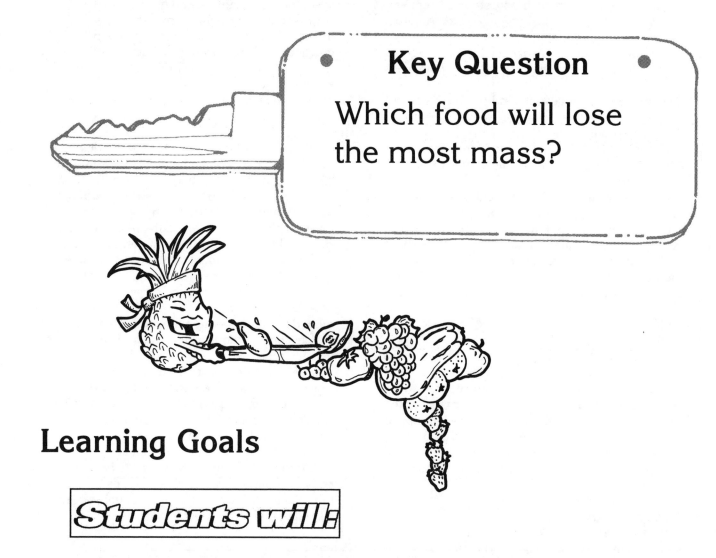

Learning Goals

Students will:

learn about the comparative amounts of water in foods.

140

CUT AND DRIED

Which food will lose the most mass? Record your predictions

Prediction	Actual
1.	1.
2.	2.
3.	3.
4.	4.
5.	5.

Record the beginning mass of each food. Multiply that by the total number of groups to find the class total mass for each food.

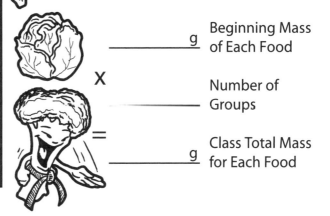

_____ g   Beginning Mass of Each Food

X   _____   Number of Groups

=   _____ g   Class Total Mass for Each Food

Record the mass for each of your group's foods after two days. Record the data from other groups. Add the mass from each group for each food to find the class total. Compare this mass to the beginning mass.

Ending Mass of Each Food

Food	A	B	C	D	E	F
Class Total						

Our Group _____

Cut and Dried

Class Totals

For each food, find the difference between beginning and ending mass. Show your work below.

Beginning Mass

Ending Mass

Each Food

All Foods

Number of Grams

Connecting Learning

1. What are we doing to keep testing conditions the same?

2. How could the results change if these controls are not used?

3. What do foods lose when they are dried?

4. Which contain more water, fruits or vegetables?

5. What food(s) do you think might beat the mass loss winner?

6. Do you think our foods still have water in them?

7. Why is the water in foods important to people?

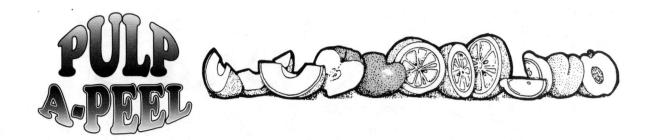

PULP A·PEEL

Topic
Edible amount in food

Key Question
How much of the _____ (chosen food) do you actually get to eat?

Learning Goal
Students will compare the edible mass of a given fruit or vegetable to its total mass.

Guiding Documents
Project 2061 Benchmark
• *Measuring instruments can be used to gather accurate information for making scientific comparisons of objects and events and for designing and constructing things that will work properly.*

NRC Standards
• *Employ simple equipment and tools to gather data and extend the senses.*
• *Objects have many observable properties, including size, weight, shape, color, temperature, and the ability to react with other substances. Those properties can be measured using tools, such as rulers, balances, and thermometers.*

NCTM Standards
• *Collect data using observations, surveys, and experiments*
• *Represent data using tables and graphs such as line plots, bar graphs, and line graphs*
• *Select and apply appropriate standard units and tools to measure length, area, volume, weight, time, temperature, and the size of angles*

Math
Measurement
    mass
Percent
Graphs

Science
Life science
    health and nutrition

Integrated Processes
Observing
Classifying
Collecting and recording data
Comparing and contrasting
Applying

Materials
For each group:
    balance
    gram masses
    calculators
    fruit or vegetable (see *Management 3*)

Background Information
Most fresh fruits and vegetables can be separated into edible and inedible parts. Edible is defined as the part we normally eat. For example, we eat the sections of grapefruit, but normally not the peeling.

Produce is generally bought by the pound. If a significant amount of the produce is inedible, it may not be the best choice for purchase unless the price per pound is low. This is something the consumer might want to consider when buying food.

Management
1. For those not ready to handle the concept and calculation of percent, have students complete the first activity page only. Then share and discuss the results as a class.
2. This activity is designed for each group to investigate a different food and then compare the edible portions of the foods. When buying the foods, record the price per pound for discussion later.
3. Each group needs a fruit or vegetable that can easily be separated into edible and inedible portions. Some suggestions include bananas, citrus, grapes, apricots, and peaches.
4. Groups of five are suggested.

Procedure
1. Ask the *Key Question*. Discuss both the parts we eat and the parts we do not eat.
2. Divide students into groups of five and distribute the first activity page. Students should write their predictions, preferably as a percent.

144

3. Have groups collect a balance, gram masses, and a fruit or vegetable.
4. After drawing it on the paper, have each group find the mass of the whole fruit or vegetable and record.
5. Instruct groups to separate the edible and inedible parts of their foods, then find the mass of each portion and record.
6. Have each group construct a graph of their data.
7. If appropriate, give students the second activity page and have them write their computation for finding the percent edible.
8. Ask groups to report thier results so they can be recorded by the class.
9. Have students complete the graph for percent edible, discuss the results, and write a conclusion.

Connecting Learning
1. What fruits and vegetables have parts we do not normally eat? [citrus, bananas, tree fruit, corn, broccoli, peppers, zucchini, melons, etc.]
2. How did your group decide which part was edible and which part was inedible? Were there any disagreements?
3. How do the edible and inedible amounts of the foods we looked at compare?
4. Which fruits and vegetables have the least waste? How do you know? How might eating habits affect the amount of waste in a fruit or vegetable? [Some people might peel their apples or pears, increasing the amount of waste. Others might eat the peel of a cucumber or carrot, reducing the amount of waste.]

5. How does the inedible mass of your group's fruit/vegetable compare with its total mass? Is this food worth the cost? (Use data on the price per pound to help evaluate.)
6. Which fruits and vegetables are the best buys?
7. What other kinds of foods have parts that we do not eat? [chicken with bones, fish (fins, head, etc), crab, un-shelled nuts]
8. Which of those foods do you think would have the most waste? Why?
9. Why should we be concerned about food waste? [amount of room available in landfills, cost of buying food, etc.]

Extensions
1. Repeat the activity with different foods.
2. Have students compute how much the edible portion actually costs.
3. Have students use the USDA's MyPyramid to classify the foods they investigated.

* Reprinted with permission from *Principles and Standards for School Mathematics,* 2000 by the National Council of Teachers of Mathematics. All rights reserved.

Key Question

How much of the chosen food do you acually get to eat?

Learning Goal

Students will:

compare the edible mass of a given fruit or vegetable to its total mass.

How much of your food can be eaten?

Prediction _____

My Group's Food

_____

Record the total mass, edible mass and inedible mass of your food.

Graph your data. Be sure to include the scale in grams.

Total Mass													
Edible Mass													
Inedible Mass													

Number of Grams

PULP A-PEEL

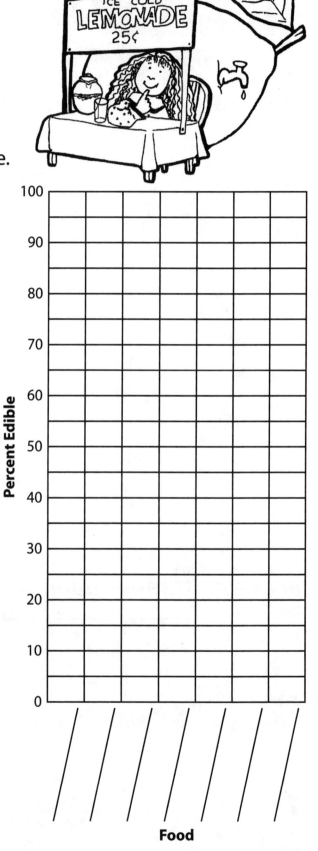

Find the percent of your food that is edible.
(edible mass ÷ total mass) x 100

Record and graph the percents for each fruit and vegetable investigated by the class.

Group	Fruit/ Vegetable	% Edible

What can you conclude about the edible portion of fruits and vegetables?

Connecting Learning

1. What fruits and vegetables have parts we do not normally eat?

2. How did your group decide which part was edible and which part was inedible? Were there any disagreements?

3. How do the edible and inedible amounts of the foods we looked at compare?

4. Which fruits and vegetables have the least waste? How do you know? How might eating habits affect the amount of waste in a fruit or vegetable?

5. How does the inedible mass of your group's fruit/vegetable compare with its total mass? Is this food worth the cost?

Connecting Learning

6. Which fruits and vegetables are the best buys?

7. What other kinds of foods have parts that we do not eat?

8. Which of those foods do you think would have the most waste? Why?

9. Why should we be concerned about food waste?

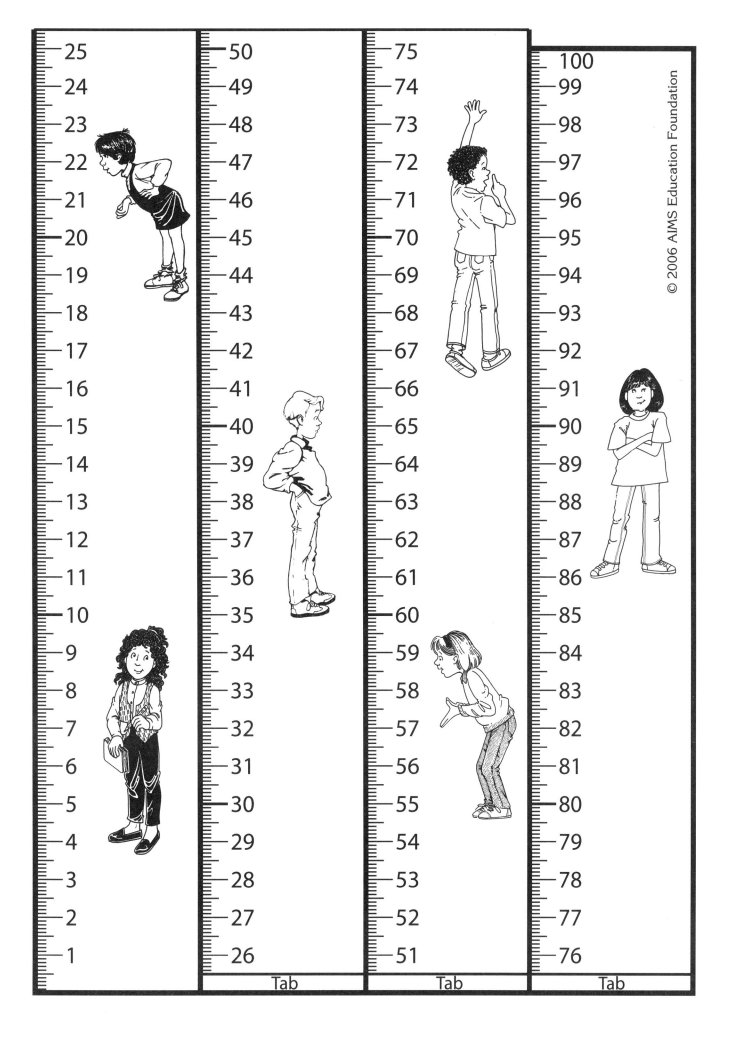

25	50	75	100
24	49	74	99
23	48	73	98
22	47	72	97
21	46	71	96
20	45	70	95
19	44	69	94
18	43	68	93
17	42	67	92
16	41	66	91
15	40	65	90
14	39	64	89
13	38	63	88
12	37	62	87
11	36	61	86
10	35	60	85
9	34	59	84
8	33	58	83
7	32	57	82
6	31	56	81
5	30	55	80
4	29	54	79
3	28	53	78
2	27	52	77
1	26	51	76
	Tab	Tab	Tab

The AIMS Program

AIMS is the acronym for "**A**ctivities **I**ntegrating **M**athematics and **S**cience." Such integration enriches learning and makes it meaningful and holistic. AIMS began as a project of Fresno Pacific University to integrate the study of mathematics and science in grades K-9, but has since expanded to include language arts, social studies, and other disciplines.

AIMS is a continuing program of the non-profit AIMS Education Foundation. It had its inception in a National Science Foundation funded program whose purpose was to explore the effectiveness of integrating mathematics and science. The project directors in cooperation with 80 elementary classroom teachers devoted two years to a thorough field-testing of the results and implications of integration.

The approach met with such positive results that the decision was made to launch a program to create instructional materials incorporating this concept. Despite the fact that thoughtful educators have long recommended an integrative approach, very little appropriate material was available in 1981 when the project began. A series of writing projects have ensued, and today the AIMS Education Foundation is committed to continue the creation of new integrated activities on a permanent basis.

The AIMS program is funded through the sale of books, products, and staff development workshops and through proceeds from the Foundation's endowment. All net income from program and products flows into a trust fund administered by the AIMS Education Foundation. Use of these funds is restricted to support of research, development, and publication of new materials. Writers donate all their rights to the Foundation to support its on-going program. No royalties are paid to the writers.

The rationale for integration lies in the fact that science, mathematics, language arts, social studies, etc., are integrally interwoven in the real world from which it follows that they should be similarly treated in the classroom where we are preparing students to live in that world. Teachers who use the AIMS program give enthusiastic endorsement to the effectiveness of this approach.

Science encompasses the art of questioning, investigating, hypothesizing, discovering, and communicating. Mathematics is the language that provides clarity, objectivity, and understanding. The language arts provide us powerful tools of communication. Many of the major contemporary societal issues stem from advancements in science and must be studied in the context of the social sciences. Therefore, it is timely that all of us take seriously a more holistic mode of educating our students. This goal motivates all who are associated with the AIMS Program. We invite you to join us in this effort.

Meaningful integration of knowledge is a major recommendation coming from the nation's professional science and mathematics associations. The American Association for the Advancement of Science in *Science for All Americans* strongly recommends the integration of mathematics, science, and technology. The National Council of Teachers of Mathematics places strong emphasis on applications of mathematics such as are found in science investigations. AIMS is fully aligned with these recommendations.

Extensive field testing of AIMS investigations confirms these beneficial results:
1. Mathematics becomes more meaningful, hence more useful, when it is applied to situations that interest students.
2. The extent to which science is studied and understood is increased, with a significant economy of time, when mathematics and science are integrated.
3. There is improved quality of learning and retention, supporting the thesis that learning that is meaningful and relevant is more effective.
4. Motivation and involvement are increased dramatically as students investigate real-world situations and participate actively in the process.

We invite you to become part of this classroom teacher movement by using an integrated approach to learning and sharing any suggestions you may have. The AIMS Program welcomes you!

AIMS Education Foundation Programs

Practical proven strategies to improve student achievement

When you host an AIMS workshop for elementary and middle school educators, you will know your teachers are receiving effective usable training they can apply in their classrooms immediately.

Designed for teachers—AIMS Workshops:
- Correlate to your state standards;
- Address key topic areas, including math content, science content, problem solving, and process skills;
- Teach you how to use AIMS' effective hands-on approach;
- Provide practice of activity-based teaching;
- Address classroom management issues, higher-order thinking skills, and materials;
- Give you AIMS resources; and
- Offer college (graduate-level) credits for many courses.

Aligned to district and administrator needs—AIMS workshops offer:
- Flexible scheduling and grade span options;
- Custom (one-, two-, or three-day) workshops to meet specific schedule, topic and grade-span needs;
- Pre-packaged one-day workshops on most major topics—only $3900 for up to 30 participants (includes all materials and expenses);
- Prepackaged four- or five-day workshops for in-depth math and science training—only $12,300 for up to 30 participants (includes all materials and expenses);
- Sustained staff development, by scheduling workshops throughout the school year and including follow-up and assessment;
- Eligibility for funding under the Title I and Title II sections of No Child Left Behind; and

- Affordable professional development—save when you schedule consecutive-day workshops.

University Credit—Correspondence Courses

AIMS offers correspondence courses through a partnership with Fresno Pacific University.
- Convenient distance-learning courses—you study at your own pace and schedule. No computer or Internet access required!

The tuition for each three-semester unit graduate-level course is $264 plus a materials fee.

The AIMS Instructional Leadership Program

This is an AIMS staff-development program seeking to prepare facilitators for leadership roles in science/math education in their home districts or regions. Upon successful completion of the program, trained facilitators become members of the AIMS Instructional Leadership Network, qualified to conduct AIMS workshops, teach AIMS in-service courses for college credit, and serve as AIMS consultants. Intensive training is provided in mathematics, science, process and thinking skills, workshop management, and other relevant topics.

Introducing AIMS Science Core Curriculum

Developed to meet 100% of your state's standards, AIMS' Science Core Curriculum gives students the opportunity to build content knowledge, thinking skills, and fundamental science processes.
- *Each* grade specific module has been developed to extend the AIMS approach to full-year science programs.
- *Each* standards-based module includes math, reading, hands-on investigations, and assessments.

Like all AIMS resources, these core modules are able to serve students at all stages of readiness, making these a great value across the grades served in your school.

For current information regarding the programs described above, please complete the following form and mail it to: P.O. Box 8120, Fresno, CA 93747.

Information Request

Please send current information on the items checked:

____ *Basic Information Packet* on AIMS materials   ____ Hosting information for AIMS workshops
____ *AIMS Instructional Leadership Program*   ____ AIMS Science Core Curriculum

Name _____ Phone _____

Address_____
        Street   City   State   Zip

AIMS Magazine

YOUR K-9 MATH AND SCIENCE
CLASSROOM ACTIVITIES RESOURCE

The AIMS Magazine is your source for standards-based, hands-on math and science investigations. Each issue is filled with teacher-friendly, ready-to-use activities that engage students in meaningful learning.

• *Four issues each year (fall, winter, spring, and summer).*

Current issue is shipped with all past issues within that volume.

| 1820 | Volume XX | 2005-2006 | $19.95 |
| 1821 | Volume XXI | 2006-2007 | $19.95 |

Two-Volume Combination

| M20507 | Volumes XX & XXI | 2005-2007 | $34.95 |

Back Volumes Available
Complete volumes available for purchase:

1802	Volume II	1987-1988	$19.95
1804	Volume IV	1989-1990	$19.95
1805	Volume V	1990-1991	$19.95
1807	Volume VII	1992-1993	$19.95
1808	Volume VIII	1993-1994	$19.95
1809	Volume IX	1994-1995	$19.95
1810	Volume X	1995-1996	$19.95
1811	Volume XI	1996-1997	$19.95
1812	Volume XII	1997-1998	$19.95
1813	Volume XIII	1998-1999	$19.95
1814	Volume XIV	1999-2000	$19.95
1815	Volume XV	2000-2001	$19.95
1816	Volume XVI	2001-2002	$19.95
1817	Volume XVII	2002-2003	$19.95
1818	Volume XVIII	2003-2004	$19.95
1819	Volume XIX	2004-2005	$35.00

Call today to order back volumes: 1.888.733.2467.

Call 1.888.733.2467 or go to www.aimsedu.org

Subscribe to the AIMS Magazine

$19.95 a year!

AIMS Magazine is published four times a year.

Subscriptions ordered at any time will receive all the issues for that year.

AIMS Online – www.aimsedu.org

For the latest on AIMS publications, tips, information, and promotional offers, check out AIMS on the web at www.aimsedu.org. Explore our activities, database, discover featured activities, and get information on our college courses and workshops, too.

AIMS News

While visiting the AIMS website, sign up for AIMS News, our FREE e-mail newsletter. Published semi-monthly, AIMS News brings you food for thought and subscriber-only savings and specials. Each issue delivers:

• **Thought-provoking articles on curriculum and pedagogy;**

• **Information about our newest books and products; and**

• **Sample activities.**

Sign up today!

AIMS Program Publications

Actions with Fractions, 4-9
Awesome Addition and Super Subtraction, 2-3
Bats Incredible! 2-4
Brick Layers II, 4-9
Chemistry Matters, 4-7
Counting on Coins, K-2
Cycles of Knowing and Growing, 1-3
Crazy about Cotton, 3-7
Critters, 2-5
Electrical Connections, 4-9
Exploring Environments, K-6
Fabulous Fractions, 3-6
Fall into Math and Science, K-1
Field Detectives, 3-6
Finding Your Bearings, 4-9
Floaters and Sinkers, 5-9
From Head to Toe, 5-9
Fun with Foods, 5-9
Glide into Winter with Math and Science, K-1
Gravity Rules! 5-12
Hardhatting in a Geo-World, 3-5
It's About Time, K-2
It Must Be A Bird, Pre-K-2
Jaw Breakers and Heart Thumpers, 3-5
Looking at Geometry, 6-9
Looking at Lines, 6-9
Machine Shop, 5-9
Magnificent Microworld Adventures, 5-9
Marvelous Multiplication and Dazzling Division, 4-5
Math + Science, A Solution, 5-9
Mostly Magnets, 2-8
Movie Math Mania, 6-9
Multiplication the Algebra Way, 4-8
Off the Wall Science, 3-9
Out of This World, 4-8
Paper Square Geometry:
    The Mathematics of Origami, 5-12
Puzzle Play, 4-8
Pieces and Patterns, 5-9
Popping With Power, 3-5
Positive vs. Negative, 6-9
Primarily Bears, K-6
Primarily Earth, K-3

Primarily Physics, K-3
Primarily Plants, K-3
Problem Solving: Just for the Fun of It! 4-9
Problem Solving: Just for the Fun of It! Book Two, 4-9
Proportional Reasoning, 6-9
Ray's Reflections, 4-8
Sense-Able Science, K-1
Soap Films and Bubbles, 4-9
Solve It! K-1: Problem-Solving Strategies, K-1
Solve It! 2nd: Problem-Solving Strategies, 2
Solve It! 3rd: Problem-Solving Strategies, 3
Spatial Visualization, 4-9
Spills and Ripples, 5-12
Spring into Math and Science, K-1
The Amazing Circle, 4-9
The Budding Botanist, 3-6
The Sky's the Limit, 5-9
Through the Eyes of the Explorers, 5-9
Under Construction, K-2
Water Precious Water, 2-6
Weather Sense: Temperature, Air Pressure, and Wind, 4-5
Weather Sense: Moisture, 4-5
Winter Wonders, K-2

Spanish Supplements*
Fall Into Math and Science, K-1
Glide Into Winter with Math and Science, K-1
Mostly Magnets, 2-8
Pieces and Patterns, 5-9
Primarily Bears, K-6
Primarily Physics, K-3
Sense-Able Science, K-1
Spring Into Math and Science, K-1

* Spanish supplements are only available as downloads from the
    AIMS website. The supplements contain only the student pages
    in Spanish; you will need the English version of the book for the
    teacher's text.

Spanish Edition
Constructores II: Ingeniería Creativa Con Construcciones
    LEGO® 4-9
    The entire book is written in Spanish. English pages not included.

Other Science and Math Publications
Historical Connections in Mathematics, Vol. I, 5-9
Historical Connections in Mathematics, Vol. II, 5-9
Historical Connections in Mathematics, Vol. III, 5-9
Mathematicians are People, Too
Mathematicians are People, Too, Vol. II
What's Next, Volume 1, 4-12
What's Next, Volume 2, 4-12
What's Next, Volume 3, 4-12

For further information write to:
AIMS Education Foundation • P.O. Box 8120 • Fresno, California 93747-8120
www.aimsedu.org • 559.255.6396 (fax) • 888.733.2467 (toll free)

Duplication Rights

Standard Duplication Rights

Purchasers of AIMS activities (individually or in books and magazines) may make up to 200 copies of any portion of the purchased activities, provided these copies will be used for educational purposes and only at one school site.

Workshop or conference presenters may make one copy of a purchased activity for each participant, with a limit of five activities per workshop or conference session.

Standard duplication rights apply to activities received at workshops, free sample activities provided by AIMS, and activities received by conference participants.

All copies must bear the AIMS Education Foundation copyright information.

Unlimited Duplication Rights

To ensure compliance with copyright regulations, AIMS users may upgrade from standard to unlimited duplication rights. Such rights permit unlimited duplication of purchased activities (including revisions) for use at a given school site.

Activities received at workshops are eligible for upgrade from standard to unlimited duplication rights.

Free sample activities and activities received as a conference participant are not eligible for upgrade from standard to unlimited duplication rights.

Upgrade Fees

The fees for upgrading from standard to unlimited duplication rights are:
- $5 per activity per site,
- $25 per book per site, and
- $10 per magazine issue per site.

The cost of upgrading is shown in the following examples:
- activity: 5 activities x 5 sites x $5 = $125
- book: 10 books x 5 sites x $25 = $1250
- magazine issue: 1 issue x 5 sites x $10 = $50

Purchasing Unlimited Duplication Rights

To purchase unlimited duplication rights, please provide us the following:
1. The name of the individual responsible for coordinating the purchase of duplication rights.
2. The title of each book, activity, and magazine issue to be covered.
3. The number of school sites and name of each site for which rights are being purchased.
4. Payment (check, purchase order, credit card)

Requested duplication rights are automatically authorized with payment. The individual responsible for coordinating the purchase of duplication rights will be sent a certificate verifying the purchase.

Internet Use

Permission to make AIMS activities available on the Internet is determined on a case-by-case basis.

• P. O. Box 8120, Fresno, CA 93747-8120 •
• permissions@aimsedu.org • www.aimsedu.org •
• 559.255.6396 (fax) • 888.733.2467 (toll free) •